CONFESSIONS OF A MALE NURSE

BY ANTHONY JAMES

Published by New Generation Publishing in 2022

First Edition

ISBN
   Paperback: 978-1-80369-451-1
   Hardback: 978-1-80369-452-8

www.newgeneration-publishing.com

New Generation Publishing

ACKNOWLEDGEMENTS

A big thank you to my darling wife Linda, for putting up with me and for listening to all my nursing stories I keep telling her. Especially for the ones I cannot put in this book.

Thanks to Josie Ward for nagging me repeatedly to put pen to paper.

Also, a massive thank you to my extremely good friends Julie (La La) Farnsworth and Louise (Dipsy) Wakefield, for being the ultimate, good and true, lifelong friends. And I'm sorry for all the pranks I have pulled on you both over the years. (Not.)

I have often been asked what it is like being a male nurse in a female-dominated profession. When I first started out in nursing, there was a stereotype that nursing was a 'female' only role. And a general prejudice of men in the role helped create a less than inclusive experience. I have been called 'gay', especially by patients, for being a male nurse, as I must be 'Gay' to want to be a male nurse. It has been a challenging experience at times. I have been treated differently to my female counterparts in that they were somehow superior nurses. There was a widespread belief that it was okay for female nurses to provide intimate care for both male and female patients. Yet, it was deemed inappropriate or perverted for male nurses to provide intimate care to a female patient, such as inserting a urethral catheter, or the giving of a bed bath. I have been told by the 'older' female nurses that men are unsuitable caregivers, as we are incapable of providing sympathy or compassionate and sensitive care. Going back to a time when PC meant a personal computer and male nurses were thin on the ground, I remember when I was introduced to my first female ward manager. She looked directly at my crotch and asked if I fainted when I got an erection.

I replied, "No, why?"

She looked me straight in the eye and said, "Well, your cock can't be that big then." She then turned and walked away to her office. Can you imagine that happening today? As a male nurse, I have had my bottom grabbed by female nurses, had sexual inuendoes to deal with. You don't get upset; you get even. It's more fun.

Women have successfully overcome the stereotype that a lot of professions are suitable only for men, such as becoming a long-distance lorry driver, playing football and rugby. Male nursing has almost overcome the same stereotype. Now I am regarded as one of the team. It's great to see in the time I have been nursing how attitudes have changed.

When you start out on your nursing career, you will discover many things, and one of those things is discovering who you really are. Finding those hidden depths and abilities you never knew you had. Some nurses will be there at birth, others will be there at the end of life, and it is a great privilege to be part of it. The joy of bringing a new life into the world, as well as being there at a difficult time for the family and patient when someone is leaving the world – both ends of life – are all treated with love, kindness and dignity. On the way, you will meet so many interesting people, both in the profession as friends and colleagues, and those you have the privilege to treat as a patient. You will touch people's lives in a way many people will not understand, and you will also be touched by those you meet and treat.

The role can be incredibly stressful at times, and as we all know, stress is bad for your mental health and wellbeing. That's why those in the profession find humour where they can. In fact, they develop a dark sense of humour that many people outside the profession don't find funny. This is our stress relief, our safety valve. Also, laughter itself is a great healer – it lightens the mood and can reduce fear in those around you and those under your care.

Love and compassion are the foundations of our profession. We offer comfort to the sick. We must be strong when you are feeling weak; we need to be brave and smile when you appear frightened. We will wipe away your tears as we hide ours. We give everything and seek nothing in return, except to watch you get better or feel safe.

Nursing is not an easy profession by any means; it will take its toll on you. It requires you to have both physical and mental stamina to make it through those gruelling shifts. But it is, at the same time, an incredibly rewarding job, especially witnessing the impact that you have on patients' lives. Not only that, but I've learnt a great deal from my patients. The elderly can teach you a lot; they are knowledgeable and sometimes incredibly funny. They have so many stories to tell and ones which we can learn from if we just take the time to listen properly.

Charles Dickens said, "Never have a heart that hardens, a temper that never tires, a touch that never hurts."

This is my favourite quote because it closely matches my destiny.

While *C.S. Lewis* said, "Hardship often prepares people for an extraordinary destiny."

Hopefully you will find most of these pages amusing, and perhaps inspiring, as you sit and read this book whilst curled up with a cup of something hot and a biscuit. As prescribed by this nurse.

CHAPTER 1

It's funny how you can make an innocent statement about what you think you could never do. Then fate appears to take over and leads your life in directions you had never imagined you would ever take.

I remember being nineteen and lying in a hospital bed after having my appendix taken out. A noise woke me shortly after midnight. I looked over to my left and saw that the nurses had drawn the curtains around the bed. They turned on the bedside lamp and they appeared to be hurrying around whilst trying to be as quiet as they could. As I looked at them rushing behind the curtain with a large trolley, I realised the person they were treating was in serious trouble and they were trying to save his life. I laid there and hoped for the best, not able to do anything else.

Later that morning, a nurse came to see how I was feeling and to administer some medication. I asked her how the chap in the bed nearby was doing; but she looked at me, closed her eyes for a moment and shook her head. I knew that she probably couldn't tell me exactly what had happened, but I knew instantly what she meant. I looked at her and said, "I could never do your job. You're all worth your weight in gold." However, fate was obviously listening to our conversation and had ideas of its own.

I was always interested in the sciences and after leaving school, my first job was working at Northern Dairies in their laboratories. I worked there until redundances were threatened because the firm was moving to another city, and they were closing the Hull plant. Outside of work, I developed a passion for photography, *no pun intended*. After being made redundant from Northern Dairies, I tried to make a living from my hobby and became a social photographer, taking portraits and photographing weddings in particular.

Big things were happening in my personal life too. I got divorced after close to thirteen years of marriage and it was hard for a few years afterwards. I wasn't able to see my two children, except on an occasional weekend. I became estranged from them for several years. It was hard, and in hindsight, I could have done better.

Though, it was while photographing a wedding that I met someone who would change the rest of my life. She had two small children when I moved in with her. The extra responsibilities meant I needed to have some extra income. The photography was not bringing in enough money and the photographic work was waning. Her name was Jane and she worked at a local hospital for a surgeon and professor. She told me that the hospital was looking for a couple of porters. I instantly said, "No way. There's no way I could work in a hospital."

Although, after about three days of thinking about it, I relented. Being a porter couldn't be that bad, surely…

I told her I would apply. Jane said, "I knew you'd come around. Your interview is next Monday."

Already, after six months, she knew me better than I knew myself. I applied for the job and was told that due to all my qualifications, I might find it more interesting to work in the operating theatres. *Oh crap!* Blood and body parts. I was not looking forward to that. But it was too late now; I could not go back on my word.

The day had come; my first day. I was extremely nervous and didn't know what to expect. They introduced me to Chris. He was the lead theatre porter, and he would be the one to train me. He showed me where the changing room was and gave me the clothes I needed to wear whilst in theatres. I had to wear theatre blues, a blue theatre head covering and a face mask. After changing into these, I went back to find Chris. He was talking to Jane; she had come to the theatres to wish me luck on my first day. I was standing next to her for about five minutes when she asked Chris where I was.

"He's right there. He's been standing next to you for five minutes," Chris said.

Jane turned to look at me and immediately burst out laughing. "Sorry, you just look so different. I didn't even recognise you!"

She wished me luck and went to get on with her own job. Chris took me on a tour of the theatres before they became occupied. There was a red line painted on the floor, and essentially those that were dressed properly and were working in the theatres could cross it. Then the strangest thing occurred. As I crossed the red theatre demarcation line, a weird feeling came over me. The only way I can describe it is that it felt like I had come home. Suddenly, when I had heard people say they had a calling, I knew exactly what they meant. I knew from that moment what I was going to do.

I was enjoying my time working in the general theatres and got along with the other two theatre porters. We collected patients and brought them to the theatre. When the theatre called, we helped take the patients to the recovery room. When fully recovered, we took them back to their ward and gave the ward a brief and basic handover of what had happened in theatre and recovery. When they had finished for the day, we would clear out the theatre rooms and give them a good clean down ready for the next day's operations.

Six months passed quickly. One of the other porters had handed his notice in as he had got a different job. Chris told me they had employed another porter to take his place and he would start the following Monday.

Monday morning came, and we had a new porter working with us. A young chap, twenty-five years old. He was so full of himself from day one, and he rubbed Chris up the wrong way from the start. He thought he knew everything about everything. If you had done something, he would say he had already done it, and better. You know the kind. He tried to tell us he could have made it as a singer, and we basically humoured him. He could *not* sing. He was told off a few times for singing loudly in the theatre rooms. Due to the echo the empty theatres produced, he must have thought he was in a recording studio and sounded good. As the week passed, we found him to be increasingly lazy and he would wander off onto the ward opposite. We watched to see what he was doing there.

It wasn't long before we noticed he kept making a beeline for the same nurse. Chris went across to the ward when the 'superstar' wasn't there and asked the nurse if he was bothering her. Apparently, she had been thinking about reporting him as she felt he was being too forward, and she was a married woman. Chris asked her to leave it until the following week so we could teach him a lesson.

We put our heads together to hatch a plan to teach our singer a lesson. I came up with an idea. We would put a card up on the requisition wall to ask the ward where the nurse worked for a certain patient's notes. The theatre used this system of request cards if we were away from the station collecting patients for theatre or taking patients back to the wards. We would take the card and action whatever needed to be done.

It was a Monday morning, and the same nurse was on duty. We waited for the theatres to quieten down before setting him up and sending him on his false mission. The card contained the ward number at the top, the patient's surname, their forename, then the reason for the request. We put the card on the wall and hid. As soon as he saw the ward number, he grabbed the card and shot off to the ward. We followed closely behind. Luckily, this particular 'job' was getting a patient onto the trolley and checking their details prior to coming across to theatre. We could see down the ward corridor as he headed straight for his favoured nurse.

He spoke to her for about thirty seconds before making his way back. We ran back and sat in the porters' room to await his arrival.

"I suppose you all think that was funny," he said.

Obviously, we pleaded innocence. "What do you mean?" I asked.

"Sending me over for this patient's notes," he replied.

"We didn't send you anywhere. Why, what happened?" Chris asked.

"I went over to the nurse and asked for Mr Jarce's notes. She said, 'Who?' I said Mr Jarce, I've come for his notes. She said they didn't have a Mr Jarce. I said, 'You must have. This card says you have a Hugh Jarce?'"

The room erupted with laughter. Not long after, the hospital's portering service gave him his marching orders. Not because of that incident though, but because of his lazy attitude and inappropriate behaviour.

I worked as a theatre porter for the next twelve months and an opportunity for a theatre Healthcare Assistant came up (HCA). I applied and got the job working in the cardiothoracic theatres. This was my biggest step yet.

Working in theatres as an HCA was incredibly interesting. By now, I had thankfully overcome my fear of blood and operations. As I would be working in the theatre during operations, and had learned what was happening, I was involved, albeit in a reduced capacity. They introduced me to the team I would work with, and I shadowed one of the more experienced HCAs for a couple of weeks. Then came my initiation. Unbeknown to me, the Operating Department Assistants (ODAs) were good at playing practical jokes on each other and any unsuspecting newbie.

I was being trained to work as the '*Dirty Nurse*', which meant that I did not assist the surgeon. That was the role of the '*Scrubbed Nurse*', who assisted the surgeon with the operation. On this day, I was assisting with an open-heart operation. It was my job to keep count of the needles, suture needles, swabs, etc., as well as fetching and carrying anything that would be required during the operation in progress. Unlike the scrubbed nurse and surgeons, I was at the foot of the patient, out of the way of everything. About a quarter of the way through the operation, I did not see the

ODA sneak up behind me. In her hands was a 60ml bladder syringe filled with ice-cold water. This was referred to as the '*Ice Rocket*'. She held it with the plunger on the floor with the nozzle of the syringe pointing upwards between my legs. Then, at an inappropriate moment, the barrel of the syringe was then thrust downwards with force. This resulted in the ice-cold water being propelled upward into my crotch. I gave out a loud gasp. Everyone turned to see what was going on.

All anyone could see were my eyes, which I could not have opened any wider, as I was still trying to catch my breath. My crotch was freezing and soaked. Someone shouted, "Welcome to the world of theatres!"

I had to stand there until I could be relieved to go and change my theatre bottoms. I could not let it go unanswered. I decided I had to plan my revenge. It has to be said that everyone worked hard and was extremely respectful and professional where the patients were concerned. However, because of the sheer nature of the job and all the bad things that come with it, I swiftly found out that you need to develop a 'nursing' sense of humour. If it was not for this release, many nurses would end up rapidly becoming burnt out mentally. I would later find out how devastating nursing can be in terms of your own health.

A couple of weeks had passed since my '*Ice Rocket*' initiation. I had been observing the ODAs and how they worked, for instance their cleaning procedure after an operation and so on. I had noticed that the female ODA would normally go for a cup of tea after the theatres had finished for the day, then come back to carry out her cleaning duties. Whilst I was cleaning down the used equipment, I noticed the stainless-steel buckets had a couple of holes in the bottom rim. I had also noticed that the inner plastic flap doors to the theatre did not always close properly.

Yes, that's right, I was going to do the old bucket above the door gag. It would have to be done safely though, as I didn't want to cause any head injuries. As I looked at the door, I saw there was a round metal conduit running above the door. My idea was to tie the bucket bottom to the conduit whilst resting the bucket on the slightly opened plastic door. I had everything within the theatre I would need. The bucket, ice-cold water, stepladders we used for cleaning, and string.

I made sure that I was the last to leave after cleaning up and everyone else had gone home for the day. I got all the equipment ready and made a few dry runs; the bucket tipped up beautifully, but next was to try it with water in. I pushed the door open with a mop handle. The water fell exactly where it needed to. I cleaned up and went home for the weekend. All I had to do was bide my time and wait for the opportunity. The day came when the female ODA was to be on the afternoon shift. I would have to move swiftly and get everything in place for when she re-entered the theatre.

After the last operation for the day had finished, I started the clean down. Eventually, everyone vacated the theatre, and I hastily set my trap. I was all set, with the ladder put back where it belonged. I left the theatre via the preparation room and made myself scarce by hiding in the next theatre.

I heard footsteps heading to the theatre. The plastic door squeaked open, then I heard a large gasp. The trap had been sprung, but then a loud deep voice shouted out, "Who the bloody hell did this?"

It was the consultant surgeon; he had returned to the theatre for his glasses. I kept my head down and denied everything. After all, I was the newbie; I didn't do things like that. The secret is I never owned up!

I worked in that theatre for about one year and it was an extremely enjoyable experience. Then I applied to university to see if could get on to the nursing course. I was thirty-four years of age and thought that I might be too old. They informed me they preferred the more mature students, as they have more life experience, which would be especially helpful in nursing. When I found out they had accepted me on the nursing course, I asked if I could transfer to the wards for some pre-nursing experience. My manager thought it would be a good idea, and although she did not want me to leave the theatre, she knew there was a vacancy on ward eighteen: admissions.

CHAPTER 2

They say that in order to survive this profession, you must have a twisted sense of humour. This is certainly true of me.

Working on the wards as an HCA gave me a good grounding for my training and gave me a better appreciation of the job the HCAs have to do every day. My new role was working on the admissions ward, ward eighteen. This gave me the greatest variety of patients coming into the hospital. My first week was to shadow one of the HCAs, working with her and learning the ropes.

The week passed swiftly. Patients came in with problems ranging from cardiac difficulties to chest infections to drug overdoses. Personally, the hardest part of the job for me at first was cleaning patients who had soiled themselves. I thought I would never get used to the smell and the cleaning up. But, after performing this essential, basic duty several times a day for a couple of weeks, it became second nature.

I was now about six weeks into the job and feeling quite confident. I had got to know a few of the patients well, those that had been on the ward for a couple of weeks. We would sit and talk for a while, share a joke or two. The ward manager was patient-orientated rather than being a task-orientated manager. She would much prefer you sitting talking to the patients when you had time, rather than sitting talking amongst ourselves.

I had got to know one chap who came onto the ward feeling poorly. After a couple of weeks, he was on the mend and was going to be discharged soon. I was taking round the tea trolley, giving the patients their afternoon drinks. I was about to ask him if he would like a drink when he suddenly started gasping for air. I asked if he was alright, but it soon became apparent he was having great difficulty breathing. I pulled the red button on the wall at the back of his bed. The alarm went off, signalling urgent help was needed straight away. I then took the metal bedhead off the bed as the rest of the staff rushed into the room and closed all the curtains. It was made up of four beds.

This provided more room for the emergency staff to work in. As one nurse was placing an oxygen mask on the patient, he grabbed my wrist. He fixed his eyes on mine, gasping for air and begging me not to let him die. "Please don't let me die, Tony. Get my wife, please." The emergency team arrived and examined him. He never took his eyes off me. Still gasping to catch his breath, he pleaded again, "Tony, please get my wife. I want to see my wife… please don't let me die."

He then passed out and his grip on my wrist loosened. I moved out of the way as the doctor started CPR and called for the defibrillator paddles. The doctors and nurses worked especially hard to save his life, but sadly it was not to be. After about forty minutes, they called it. My heart felt heavy, and a cold shiver ran down my spine. I had failed him. He died without seeing his wife one more time. This was the first time I had ever witnessed this, and it reduced me to tears. It was the worst feeling in the world.

The ward manager was excellent. She took me into the office, made me a cup of coffee and counselled me brilliantly. She explained everything they did and why they did it. The manager and the staff were fantastically supportive and looked after me for the rest of the week. I knew this was something I would unfortunately get to see a lot of. He had suffered a pulmonary embolism, which had caused a cardiac arrest. The manager asked if I would like to help with the 'last offices', as this is the last compassionate and caring duty you can do for the deceased. She said that I should talk to him as though he was still alive and follow the other nurse's lead.

This entailed carefully washing the body, placing the body in a shroud, combing his hair, and finally wrapping the body up. It was customary on the ward to cover the face last. As they did, they always said goodnight and said the patient's name. Once again, this reduced me to tears. This was the hardest thing I had ever done. It still haunts me to this very day, and I still feel I let that patient down.

A couple of months passed by without incident. The ward manager varied my job as an HCA, since I was going to train to become a fully trained staff nurse. I was enjoying it immensely. Part of my role was to help transport the patients to other wards as beds became available. This was in addition to the obvious making beds, helping patients wash and dress and going around with the drinks trolley. On the ward, we also had a housekeeper. He was always upbeat, friendly, funny and incredibly camp. Everyone loved him, from the nursing staff to the patients. He was a popular and necessary member of the ward team. I recall one afternoon; I was sitting at the nurses' station doing some paperwork when he was stood between the kitchen area and the nurses' station. "Oh my God, oh my God!" he exclaimed.

"What's the matter?" I asked.

"Look, look in the kitchen! Bubbles… there are bubbles everywhere," he said in an incredibly funny manner, flailing his arms dramatically. I looked through the kitchen door window… the kitchen was about two feet deep in bubbles! By now, other staff members had come to see what the commotion was all about. One by one, they peered into the kitchen before bursting into fits of laughter.

"What have you done?" asked the ward manager.

"I couldn't find the dishwasher tablets, so I used the fairy liquid," he replied.

The manager pressed her lips together to stop herself from laughing. As she turned to walk away, she said, "I hope you have a large mop and bucket."

It took a couple of hours to clear up all the bubbles, which incidentally, from that day, became his nickname – chosen by himself, I might add. It was a Tuesday morning; we had washed and dressed all the patients that needed help to do so. We had made all the beds, and breakfast had been served. It was now around 09:15.

The emergency alarm sounded. We ran to help and closed the curtains. The cardiac arrest was the patient in bed one. The emergency staff did everything they could to save him. Unfortunately, they could not. A short time later, we performed last offices and the porters came to take the body to the mortuary. It was about an hour later when someone sounded the alarm again. It was the same room. This time it was the patient in bed two. Again, they did everything possible to save his life. Once again, sadly, the person could not be saved. We performed our necessary duties, and the porters came and took him to the mortuary. It was shortly after lunch when the emergency alarm sounded again.

As we ran into the same room, another HCA was taking the bedhead off from bed three. We drew the curtain around the remaining patient in bed four. The emergency team tried for roughly forty minutes without success to save him. They did not want to give up on any patient, as losing a patient is the worst thing that can happen. I could see the disappointment and hurt in their faces as they again, reluctantly, called the time of death.

For the third time that day, we performed last offices, said goodnight to the deceased patient and sent him to the mortuary. Some thirty minutes after the body left the ward, a patient pressed a call button, and I went off to see what the patient needed. It was the man in bed four of that room. He said, "I don't want to sound insensitive, but I have just watched those three men die in number order coming around the room. Please… can they move me to another room? I don't want to be the fourth." We moved him straight away to another room. He did not become the fourth, and fortunately, no one else died that day.

The following week, we had a young student join us for her first placement. And as with all young first students, she was keen, so as soon as she saw the blue lights of the ambulance, she was off up the corridor to greet it. One particular time, we had advance notice of a 'blue-light' admission. The ward manager and I were walking up the corridor when we saw the ambulance arriving. We continued to the entrance doors when the student joined us. The student opened the door to allow the ambulance crew to push the old lady in a wheelchair onto the ward.

"You look nice and cosy," said the student nurse. "You're all wrapped up tight like a little clitoris," she added.

The ward manager looked at me, then we looked at the student nurse, who was clearly oblivious to her statement.

The ambulance man looked at the old lady, then looked at us, shook his head and said, "I think she meant a chrysalis."

CHAPTER 3

I applied to Hull University's nursing course and was successful. As it transpired, I was one of only four males out of a cohort of about one hundred and eighty nursing students. I would start the three-year course that September. It would be the first course of its kind **not** to have any exams. There would be lots of written assignments at the end of each course. Perfect, because I hated exams. At least you could research and have someone read the essay before you handed it in. I made good friends with Adam, one of the other students. We appeared to have a lot in common, especially our sense of humour. This would come into play a few times during the three years.

We studied hard and helped each other during our first few essays. Then the Christmas break came and went. It was now the second week of March, and we were planning an April fools' prank. We agreed to do it at the end of March, as doing it on April the first would probably give it away too easily. We drafted a notice stating that because of the high level of education needed, the education board had retracted the 'no exams' decision and we would have to have a couple of full days dedicated to exams. We pinned it to the notice board at about quarter to nine. By nine o'clock, everyone was talking about it and saying how unfair it was and that not much notice had been given to prepare for these exams.

We sat in the lecture theatre listening to the outrage, and we too verbalised our disapproval at this decision and egged people on to demand an explanation from the tutors. We of course denied having anything to do with the notice and showed indignation at being accused of doing so. The lecturer walked into the room and the cohort proceeded to pound her with question after question regarding the notice that there would be exams for two days during the following week. The lecturer stood there, stunned by all the questions and unhappy students. She said she would look into it and report back to us in the second period. The second period came, and the lecturer informed everyone that the notice must be a prank as there were no exams planned at any future time. The relief amongst the students was palpable. It's still unclear why people suspected me and Adam of being responsible. We believed we both looked like butter wouldn't melt in our mouths. Or so we thought…

It was time for us to have our first nursing placement. They allocated me to spend four weeks with the traffic police in Beverley. The first week went by swiftly. It was a great experience, especially when we rushed to a call with the blues and twos blaring out. One of our first calls was to a sudden death. A young man in his early thirties had dropped dead in the kitchen. The police had to attend to rule out any suspicious circumstances of a sudden death. The ambulance crew was already there by the time we arrived. The police officer spoke with the ambulance crew and then the parents of the young man. He was visiting his parents and was making a cup of tea when he had suddenly died.

The ambulance crew stated they could find nothing to explain it and would have to wait for a post-mortem examination to determine the cause. We stayed until the 'private ambulance' arrived to take the body away. We made sure the family was alright and got a neighbour to come and sit with them for a while before we left. We would later find out the poor man had suffered a massive heart attack and had died instantly.

The following week, I worked the afternoon shift with the traffic police. Jane had asked me to call in at the bank on my way and deposit some cash for her. She gave me her cheque book and I paid in the money. It was merely a ten-minute walk from the bank to the police station. I was due to go out with the same officer that afternoon; we went to the car and checked it over inside and out, then left the station. It was a relatively quiet shift, with the occasional speeding and parking fines handed out. The shift was now over. I grabbed my coat from the back seat and proceeded to walk home.

The next day, I was about to set off for the police station for another afternoon shift with the traffic police when the phone rang. I answered the phone.

"Hello, can I speak with Anthony James, please?"

"Hi, that's me."

"Hello, it's the Beverley traffic police. How are you doing?"

"I'm fine. How can I help?"

"You were out with Officer Kent yesterday, is that right?"

"Yes, we were out in the afternoon. I am out with him again this afternoon. Is there something wrong?"

"Can you tell me if you lost anything yesterday?"

"I don't think so. I appear to have everything with me."

"Are you sure?"

I checked everything. At that point, Jane entered the room. She asked if I still had her cheque book.

"Hello, erm… I might have dropped my partner's cheque book in the back of the police car."

"Can you confirm her name for me, please?"

"Jane Smith."

"I have it here. We'll explain everything when you get here this afternoon."

I thought no more about it and set off to the police station. When I arrived, one of my fellow students greeted me with a large grin.

"So, you're the reason we're getting off late."

"I don't know what you mean?"

"This morning, we arrested a couple of shoplifters, put them in the back of the car, and drove them here. The officer did a routine check of the car to see if they had ditched anything in the back. He found your cheque book. He questioned them for ages, thinking they had stolen it and tried to hide it under the seat. They admitted to shoplifting but wouldn't admit to stealing the cheque book."

"Oops, I hadn't realised it had fallen out of my coat pocket."

The police officer entered the tearoom.

"Sorry about that. I was merely trying to help you fit up a couple of shoplifters," I said jokingly.

"We do not 'fit up' anyone at this police station," said the chief superintendent as he walked into the room.

Embarrassed, I hung my head down and apologised. He just gave me one of those looks that puts you in your place. During my four weeks with the traffic police, we had attended one sudden death, one hanging by suicide, one car crash at a local spot renowned for collisions, several speeding offences and a suspected caravan theft. The only downside was losing the cheque book and being reprimanded by the chief superintendent, oops! It was an enjoyable and eye-opening experience that passed all too fleetingly. It did, however, highlight the everyday experiences the police need to deal with.

My next placement would not be as enjoyable. After spending time back at the university, it was time for my first ward placement. They sent me to a local hospital on an elective surgical ward. My first shift was a late shift, starting at one o'clock and finishing at nine o'clock. I had been on the ward about ten minutes when a young student nurse walked past me in floods of tears. I went after her to see what the matter was. She was nineteen and had never been on a ward before. She told me she was not planning on staying and would report something to her personal tutor. I wondered what had upset her so much. I was about to find out.

The ward manager met me at the nurses' station and allocated my mentor. She asked me what experience I had, so I told her my background working at this hospital, but on the medical side, I had none on the surgical wards. She said my theatre experience would be especially helpful. I asked her about the student that had left the ward in tears. She too hadn't been on shift long and didn't know a student had left in tears. I did not give it a second thought as I had to help get a couple of patients ready for theatre. After that, we saw to the patients that had come back from theatre, made them comfortable and administered any pain relief that they needed. My mentor informed me she would be off for the next two days and would introduce me to the nurse that would look after me instead.

We took our next patient down to theatre and handed her over to the theatre staff, returned to the ward and caught up with some paperwork. Sue, the nurse who I would be working with, walked past the nurses' station.

"Sue, this is Tony. He will work with you for two days while I'm off."

"Great," was all she said before walking away.

After finishing the paperwork, we had another patient to pick up from surgery and bring back to the ward. We made her comfortable, and I went to make her a cup of tea. On the way, I passed Sue, and said hello again. She mumbled something and kept on walking; I thought she was just too busy to chat, so I carried on with my tasks. The rest of the shift passed uneventfully. It was now time to give a 'handover' to the night shift. My mentor gave me the responsibility of giving the handover of her patients as I was used to it from working as an HCA.

I arrived early for shift the next afternoon and sat having a coffee waiting for the 'handover' from the morning shift. Sue came into the dayroom, and I said hello. She mumbled something and left. The rest of the afternoon, staff came in with their drinks and waited for the handover. They asked me who I was, what year student I was and who I was working with. One of them said, "Oh, really? Good luck."

I thought she was teasing me. Though I was about to find out why that young student nurse ran off the ward crying the day before. We completed handover and before I could ask anything, Sue got up and walked out. I could see by the faces of the other nurses smirking that this was going to be an interesting shift. I finally caught up with Sue in the four-bedded area. I asked her what she wanted me to do. She spoke normally, then got quieter and quieter until the end of the sentence was merely a mumble. I asked her to repeat what she had said as I didn't catch all of it. She did the same thing again. I told her I couldn't understand what she was saying.

"Are you deaf?!" she shouted.

"No, but please speak normally, then I can understand you."

"Just get on with it!" she said sharply, before walking away.

One patient sitting by his bed then said, "Looks like you're next."

I asked him to explain. "She was like this with the young nurse yesterday. She ran off crying."

I said, "Thank you for the heads-up."

Remembering what had been done yesterday with my mentor, I looked at the board to see if we had any patients attending theatre that afternoon. There was no one scheduled for theatre that afternoon, however. So, I put my HCA head on and asked our patients if there was anything I could do for them.

Sue came back and said, "Well!"

"Well what?" I replied.

"Have you done what I asked you to do?"

"I don't know what you have asked me to do."

Another nurse came over for a countersignature on a drug card. While she was there, I asked Sue what it was she had wanted me to do.

"You can't believe the level of students we're getting," she said to the other nurse. She then turned to me and said, "I asked you to tidy out the linen cupboard as we have had a delivery and it needs putting away."

"Ah, that's what you were mumbling. No, I haven't. Shall I do it now?" I said with a note of sarcasm and headed off to sort the linen cupboard out.

She was like this for the whole placement when no one was around to hear her mumbling her requests. I decided she had now picked on the wrong person. They had bullied me for most of my senior years at school, but no more. I promised myself when I left school that no one would bully me ever again. I even went and learned karate, which had given me more confidence than anything. Luckily though, I have never had to use it.

I now made a diary of everything she did, from mumbling her orders to me to the way she spoke to other students on the ward. Then one day, I struck gold. I was working at the nurses' station when she asked the ward manager to countersign some intravenous fluids that she had written on the fluids sheet. The manager countersigned them and said loud enough for me to hear, "Next time, it would be better to get the doctor to write up the fluids." Time, date and reason went straight into my diary.

My four-week placement was now over. I received a glowing report from my mentor, stating that I had applied myself well, and received good feedback from the patients we were looking after. She apologised for Sue's behaviour, saying that staff had tried to report her in the past, but she appeared to be Teflon coated. I replied that I was not finished with her yet. The ward manager walked past the nurses' station, and I asked if I could have a word with her before I left. I discussed Sue's behaviour with the ward manager. She asked me why it had taken so long for me to come forward. I said that I had wanted to get my facts right and to make sure it was not merely a clash of personalities. Also, I wanted enough evidence to make a proper case. The ward manager asked what I wanted to be done. I said all I wanted at that stage was for her behaviour to be brought to her attention and for her to attend a communications programme, along with an anti-bullying education programme. We left it at that, and I thanked her for my time on the ward.

Around two weeks after my placement, I was sitting in the lecture theatre when someone entered and spoke to the lecturer.

"Anthony James. Do we have an Anthony James present?"

I put my hand up.

"Can you please see your personal tutor right away?"

I knocked on his door and was invited to enter. "This is Margaret Blanchard from the RCN." (RCN was the Royal College of Nursing.)

"Hello."

"Please sit," my personal instructor said.

"What can I do for you?" I asked, thinking this was going to be some sales pitch for joining the union.

"I am representing Sue Collins, a staff nurse on the ward where you had your last placement."

I looked at her suspiciously and said, "Go on."

"She is putting an official complaint in against you for falsely accusing her of bullying and reporting her to the ward manager."

I chuckled as I looked at my personal tutor, then looked back at her.

"I cannot see what could be amusing you. Sue has requested that you are to be dismissed from the nursing course."

I was getting extremely annoyed that this nurse was now trying to deflect negative attention back onto me. My slight grin now turned into a large smile as I stared back at her.

"Okay, if that's how she wants to play this, I have already discussed this matter with my personal tutor and logged everything in my journal. I want to end this meeting now, and we will resume with a member of the NMC present." (NMC stood for the Nursing and Midwifery Council.)

"I don't think there's a need to go that far," she replied.

"Really? Let me enlighten you. Your client *is* a bully. She would start speaking and get quieter and quieter until she basically mumbled, then when you asked her what she had said, she would loudly say, practically shouting, are you deaf and stupid? She upset a young student nurse who, after being on the ward about an hour, left sobbing and did not return. Is Sue a prescriber?"

"I'm not sure," she replied.

"Let me enlighten you; no, she is not. I have evidence of her prescribing fluids for a patient. I have the patient's name, who gave me permission to use her name, as well as the time and date of the incident. Even the ward manager, when she countersigned the fluid prescription, said it would be better in future if she got a doctor to write up and sign for the fluids. So, please go back to this nurse and inform her I have a letter addressed to the NMC with all the details in there. And that I am seriously contemplating sending it."

"Sorry, I know nothing about this," the woman replied.

"Then you can inform her I expect her to be attending the courses I suggested to the ward manager, and if I hear a single student complain or even suggest she has tried to bully them, I will send the information off to the NMC."

I was fuming.

"That sounds like a threat."

"Take it any way you like. I will not stand for any bullying. All I wanted was for her to have her behaviour brought to her attention and for her to attend a couple of courses to help improve her behaviour. But she obviously still wants to bully or intimidate me by stating she wants me thrown off this nursing course. Please inform her that; one, they will not be throwing me off this course as I have done nothing wrong; and two, I am merely a stamp away from posting my information to the NMC and I'm sure they will throw her out of nursing. So, if she wants to remain in her career, she will attend those courses and mend her ways."

My personal tutor sat there, listening. He could see I was becoming, shall we say, 'passionate' about the situation.

"I have seen the report that his mentor has given him for this placement; it was outstanding. We encourage students to speak out against bullying and any bad practice. Tony has already told me he left it in the hands of the ward manager to deal with her through education. Please go back to your lecture, Tony, and I will see you again after lunch."

He winked and sat back in his chair. I later found out from the student 'grapevine' that Sue had become, as one student described, "sickly nice".

CHAPTER 4

It was now my second year of nursing school. I had remained on the '*nursing bank*' so I could still work as an HCA on weekends or after university to earn some extra cash. I had done a few shifts on ward twenty-two, a chest ward, which would be my next placement. I was looking forward to it as I knew and got on well with the nursing team on the ward. The first week flew past. My mentor was due to be off during the second week. So, they allocated me another person to look after me during the second week. A staff nurse called Kath that used to work nights was now doing a couple of mornings during the week.

She was designated the role of teaching me the '*drug round*', in other words, how to dispense and administer the medications safely. It was time for the drug round one morning, so I made my way to the nurses' station and unlocked the drug trolley from the wall. Kath appeared from around the corner and took control of the drug trolley. As we entered the first room, and before I could ask anything, she immediately snapped her fingers and pointed to a clear sputum pot on the patient's table, then flicked her hand and finger, which signalled I was to take it away. I removed the pot and replaced it with an empty one. I then asked if I could dispense the medications and for her to double-check them to make sure I was doing it correctly. This is how I had done it with my mentor. She replied with a resounding 'no'. She clicked her fingers and pointed at the other sputum pots and told me to get rid of them.

I replaced all of them with fresh, empty ones. Kath was now in the second room, and as I entered (you might have guessed), she again clicked her fingers and pointed to the sputum pots. I cleared that room of pots also, replacing them with empty ones. Then I went into the other two rooms and replaced the used pots for clean, empty ones. I was now ahead of her.

"Do you want me to take over and you check what I do?" I asked.

I was confident of an answer of yes, but instead, she said, "You can empty the catheter bags now."

"I can do those after the drug round," I said.

"You can do them now."

I didn't argue. I merely got on with the job she asked me to do. I couldn't help thinking that some nurses' attitudes needed adjusting. I found another nurse to work with, which went well. We had a couple of new arrivals, which I could admit to the ward. The rest of the morning was helping with patient care, checking the fluid balance sheets and other general duties that needed to be done.

After lunch, I hurriedly ran around changing sputum pots and catheter bags. Surely, I thought, I could now do the drug round and Kath could check my progress. This was part of my workbook and would need to be signed off at the end of my placement; therefore, all the experience I received would contribute to a better result.

I met up with Kath as she was about to go into the first room. On entering the room, she noticed that a patient had used their sputum pot. She clicked her finger and wagged it again. I asked her politely not to click her fingers as I found it rude and unnecessary. She stared at me as though I had asked her for a thousand pounds. However, I exchanged the sputum pot and followed her around whilst she dispensed the medications, and I handed them to the patients. After the drug round, I had a quiet word with one of the other nurses about my experience with Kath. She informed me Kath hated working days and sometimes acted like this.

Kath was on shift again the following day. She obviously ignored my request to not click her fingers at me as that is exactly what she did on the morning drug round yet again. The first room we went in, she clicked and wagged her finger at the sputum pots. One of the HCAs witnessed this when she entered the room. The HCA followed me into the sluice room and explained Kath would not touch the sputum pots and had clicked her fingers at her previously as well.

I decided I would confront Kath later. In the meantime, I helped the HCA with her duties. I considered the possibility of making a complaint against her, as I did with the nurse on my first placement. This was a form of bullying and there is no place for it anywhere, especially in a healthcare setting. For the third day in a row, I had Kath showing me the drug round. I decided not to bother protesting. I would let her get on with it and I would find something else to do. I would have to have a word with the ward manager in the afternoon when she came on duty.

By that time, we had washed and dressed the patients, made their beds and served breakfast. It was now close to ten o'clock. I was in the main corridor when the catering lady came along with the food for that day's lunch. As she pushed her trolley past me, I noticed a large jug of something.

"What's in that?" I asked.

"It's leek and potato soup. It needs diluting and heating for lunch."

I had an idea. "Can I steal a couple of teaspoons full of the cold soup, please?"

"Sure, what for?"

"I'll tell you later," I replied as I took a small sample of the cold soup.

It was time for the morning drug round. Kath had collected the drug trolley, and I followed her into room one. As predicted, Kath spotted the sputum pots on the patient's tables and yet again clicked her fingers and wagged them at me in order to remove them. I sneaked the pot of cold leek and potato soup out of my pocket and pretended to pick it up off the table of bed one.

"Kath, is this lady on antibiotics?" I asked.

"No," came the short reply.

"Well, looking at this sputum, it looks like it's infected," I said as I unscrewed the lid. Her eyes widened as she watched me sniff the sample pot.

"It smells infected," I said as I then placed a finger inside the pot, stirred it around, then pulled my finger out. She watched in absolute horror as I then sucked the cold soup off my finger. Her face turned a strange colour as she placed her hand over her mouth and ran off, retching.

I waited by the drug trolley until she returned. I looked at her and said, "I told you about clicking your fingers at me. Never do it again."

Word soon spread about what I had done, as one of the HCAs had witnessed it and couldn't wait to tell the other staff members about it. Yet, when the ward manager found out about it later that afternoon, she summoned me to her office. She asked me why I had done it. I explained that I had asked Kath not to click her fingers at me on two separate occasions.

"I'm here to learn; I have worked for you on this ward for the last six months as an HCA after university and on weekends; I have never disrespected you or any member of your staff. I do not expect to be disrespected either, as a student or as an HCA."

She shook her head, laughed and said that, unofficially, she wished she had seen it, as she was already aware of how Kath had been treating me as someone had spoken up on my behalf. The manager said she would have a word with Kath about her attitude before she left for the day.

The next morning, during handover, Kath gave me a look that seemed to show that the ward manager had spoken to her. She did not look happy. I had admitted one of our new patients with a severe chest infection; he was also on Methadone. Kath did the morning drug round, and again, I handed out what she dispensed. She politely asked me to go to the controlled drug cupboard with her. I countersigned a dose of Methadone out of the controlled drug cabinet. Kath instructed me to make sure he drank it there and then, and to make sure the patient consumed a glass of water after taking it. I took the Methadone along to the patient and instructed him to take it then and consume a glass full of water. He did as I asked and thanked me.

On the afternoon drug round, again Kath asked me to countersign the Methadone out of the controlled cupboard.

Again, she asked me to make sure the patient took it straight away and drank another glass of water after taking it.

On finishing the drug round, we walked by the single room where this young man on Methadone was staying, but he was not in his room. Kath noticed a medication pot on his table with a green liquid in it. The ward manager happened to be coming down the corridor at the same time.

"I thought I told you to make sure he took the Methadone. This is a controlled drug and should not be lying around unattended where anyone could get hold of it," said Kath, making it obvious to the ward manager that there had been a potential mistake.

The manager asked, "Why have you left a controlled drug unattended?"

I looked at her with a cheeky smile and replied, "That's his Corsodyl mouthwash."

I went into the room and brought it out for them to examine; it was indeed Corsodyl mouthwash. Kath's face was a picture of embarrassment. I smiled and walked away.

All too often, we underestimate the power a simple touch has on a person. We had an elderly lady on the ward who was extremely poorly. She could not even lift a spoon to feed herself. They gave me the privilege of helping to look after her as part of my training. I used to feed her breakfast and lunch, help to change her bed linen, and clean her up. She was often teary as she had once been an extremely independent and proud lady before her hospital stay. We would tell her not to worry, and that it was our job to look after her, and to help make her better again.

She had been on the ward about two weeks and was not getting any better. One morning straight after handover, we were helping to get the patients out of bed, as well as taking those who could wash themselves a bowl of warm water and a towel. After this, we washed and dressed those that needed help. This lady was doubly incontinent. She lay in bed with tears rolling down her face. The HCA drew the curtains around her and wiped away her tears. I helped to clean her up, wash her and change her bed linen. We asked if she wanted to be sat up. She shook her head slightly. We made her as comfortable as we could and gave her breakfast. She hardly ate anything and made a slight wave with her hand to say that she had eaten enough.

As I placed her hands into a comfortable position, she looked at me and smiled whilst at the same time she held my hand and gently patted it. I smiled back and gave her a cheeky wink. She was saying thank you the only way she could. She died sleeping about an hour later.

Compassion and love are the foundation of nursing. We dispense this regularly. We are supposed to be strong when the weak cannot be.

There is a quote by Christina Feist-Heilmeier, RN:

"*Every nurse was drawn to nursing because of a desire to care, to serve, or to help.*"

Maybe this is what I had felt that first day as a porter working in the theatres.

Later that afternoon, I was asked if I would take a blood pressure reading of an eighty-year-old lady admitted for investigations. I wheeled the blood pressure machine to the patient. She was in a four-bedded area, and she was in bed three. The only other patient was a young woman admitted with breathing problems, and she was in bed one.

As I approached her bed, I could see she was on intravenous fluids, and the stand was on the right side of the bed near the window.

"Hello, Betty. I need to take your blood pressure. Is that alright?"

"Yes, love, help yourself."

As I took her left arm from under the bedcover, I noticed that someone had put her on a long line, which started at the fluid bag on her right side, down under her pillow and into her left arm.

"Sorry, Betty, but I will need to use your right arm, as this one has your fluids going into it."

"That's okay, son, you can lean over. Save having to pull the bed away from the window."

"Thank you, if you can just lift your right arm for me."

She lifted her right arm barely enough for me to get the cuff around her arm. As I did, she suddenly grabbed my testicles with her left hand and held on tight. I was dancing around on the spot, gently trying to remove her hand, but she didn't seem to have any intention of letting go.

"Oh, oh," I squeaked.

I then noticed the lady in bed one struggling to breathe and clutching at her chest.

"Quick, let go. The lady needs help."

Betty thankfully let go and I ran to give this lady her oxygen mask, which had fallen off the bed. After a few good deep breaths of oxygen, the lady looked over at the old lady and smiled.

"You're a daft old bat. Are you trying to kill me? I've never seen anything so funny."

"Are you alright?"

"Yes, I'm fine now. I suddenly burst out laughing and it took my breath away."

As I went back to Betty, she drew back the bedcover and said, "Now that we've been acquainted, would you like to get in?"

I didn't know where to put myself. For the duration of her stay, she told us no end of jokes and funny stories. She was a lovely lady with a fantastic sense of humour, although she could be seen as being a bit inappropriate at times. I like to think she was merely living her life to the max.

CHAPTER 5

I was now in my third and final year. The previous two years had flown past. One more year and I would be a registered nurse, so long as I passed that year's assignments. My next essay was on health and wellbeing. Everyone was doing the expected. I wanted to do something different. My next placement was on the elective surgery ward. I knew one nurse, Julie, on that ward incredibly well and also knew she had applied to be a lecturer at the university. I decided I would run my idea past her and get her to assess my essay before handing it in.

A couple of recent lectures had been about healthy living and eating a well-balanced diet in order to maintain good health. I now had an idea for my essay. I would write my essay on the homeless and their nutrition. It is fine advising everyone to eat the best quality food and eat lots of fruit and vegetables, though what if you couldn't afford to eat healthily? I thought I would visit homeless shelters and seek information, as well as interview any homeless people that would talk to me about their situation.

Whilst on placement, I ran this idea past my mentor and later that day I ran it past my partner Jane. They both thought it was a good angle, so I researched it and began writing it. I made an appointment to visit a local homeless shelter to find out what they offered the homeless. They informed me that the doors opened at a specific time, and the homeless people had to leave the shelter at a set time in the morning. The homeless had to find their own things to do between these times. The shelter also informed me they relied heavily on food donations from charities and local stores.

It was relatively hit and miss what they had to eat, but the experienced kitchen staff made it as healthy and as well balanced as they could. I interviewed a few of the homeless people who used the shelter. We discussed healthy eating and food nutrition. I was told that they preferred hot pizza and a hot bag of chips over a healthy meat salad sandwich or any other healthier option. This was because the hot food kept them feeling warmer when it was cold, especially if they had to sleep rough if the shelter was full.

I collected and sorted all my research notes and wrote my essay. This felt like my best essay to date. After writing it, I asked Julie if she would read it and offer any helpful criticism. After moving a couple of paragraphs about and altering the odd sentence, she said it was a good essay. I put her on the spot and asked if she was marking it, what would she score it? She said she would give it high eighties to low nineties. My face lit up. Top marks indeed. The following week, I handed my essay in to be marked.

Since it was my third year, they gave me a six-bedded room to look after. I needed to plan patients' care, get them ready for theatre, then look after them post-op. I was feeling like a fully-fledged nurse, albeit under supervision and under the incredibly watchful eye of my mentor. Monday morning of the second week, at handover, they informed me we had a first-year student to look after too. She was nineteen and had never set foot on a ward before; I remembered the other young student from my first placement. I would give her a better experience than the other poor student had received.

We were an HCA down as one rang in sick that morning. The student was exceptionally keen and wanted to get stuck in. She was supposed to be supernumerary but said she wanted to play an active part. My six patients were due for theatre during the morning, so all of them were nil-by-mouth. I asked the student if it was alright if she made sure they all had a shower and dressed in their theatre gowns and paper knickers ready for theatre. They were all self-caring and on the ward for elective operations. I said I would help the nurse in the next six-bedded area as they had all had their operations yesterday and would need some help. She said yes; I told her where the linen cupboard was and said if she needed any help, she could come and find one of us.

She appeared extremely confident for a young student, especially one that had not been on a ward before. I had told her what to do, so off I went to help my mentor with her post-op patients. After about an hour, she came to find me and proudly announced that they had all showered and the beds had been stripped. Then she said, "Your theatre gowns are posh."

I looked at her and said, "They're like all the other theatre gowns. What do you mean posh?"

"They've all got posh frilly collars."

My mentor looked at me and her eyes widened, but we said nothing aloud. Our faces said it all. *Oh no*, I thought as we went to investigate.

We stood in the doorway and looked in the room. All six patients were sitting upright, looking at each other expressionless. They looked smart, albeit in their posh white shrouds. I ran to the linen cupboard and retrieved six theatre gowns.

"Use these. Those ones they're wearing are for special occasions."

Me and my mentor slinked away hastily and were crying with laughter at the poor student's mistake. Later that morning, when we explained what she had done, she was mortified. We explained it was alright, no harm had been done and even the six men thought it was hilarious when we apologised and explained the poor student's unfortunate mistake. The young student double-checked everything after that.

The rest of the placement went by without a hitch. I thoroughly enjoyed it and learned a lot about the responsibility you have as a staff nurse.

Back at university, it was time to get the results of my essay. I was looking forward to a high eighties mark for the first time. Then I saw the result – WHAT? Forty-two percent!

I went in search of the tutor who marked my paper. I found her in her office.

"Hi, can I have a word, please?"

"Sure, come in. What can I do for you?"

"My essay – you marked it at forty-two percent. This must be a mistake. My lowest mark so far was fifty-eight percent."

"Ah yes, I was expecting a visit. I tried my hardest to fail you. I even gave it to another tutor to mark, hoping she could fail it."

"Why? I was told that it was a good essay and should achieve my highest mark yet."

"We are not interested in what the homeless cannot afford to do. We are not interested in the poor and what they can barely afford. We are interested in what can be done, what we can promote. You can put in an objection to the marking, but I'll tell you it will not do you any good. We could not fail it because it met all the criteria needed for the essay, so I gave it the lowest possible pass mark."

You bitch, I thought to myself, wanting to blurt it out. I stormed out of her office and went straight to see my personal tutor. He disagreed with the marking but said it was her who had set the essay and it was up to her how she marked it. I was fuming.

My next placement was with the community mental health team. They introduced me to my mentor, Dave. The first thing he did was have a look at my workbook to see which experiences I needed from my placement. I was still fuming over my last essay and related the story to him. He looked up from my workbook and said, "So, they just want the utopian versions. That is not a problem. Let's give it to them."

"What do you mean?"

"What's your next essay on?"

"Mental health. The criterion for the essay is there," I said, pointing to the page.

"Right, sit here, pen and paper at the ready. It says laws surrounding mental health. Okay. It has to be completely anonymous, yes?"

"Yes."

"Superb. Let's have a client standing on a garage roof exposing himself and urinating on passers-by. Then we will get the police involved. Next, he tries urinating on the police, which will get him arrested. He's a known schizophrenic and the police have had him sectioned for assessment. He is refusing his medications and becoming more unstable, so under the law and with him being sectioned, we can forcibly administer drugs for his own good. Right, that'll get you started. You just need to research schizophrenia. I'll give you the legal information. There you are. We've practically written your essay to their utopian standards, and because it is anonymous, they cannot argue it's not real."

"That was amazing, thank you."

"If that's all they are interested in, then give it to them."

The placement was especially interesting. During my second week, we had to visit a mother and son who were on the run from aliens. I did not say what I was thinking and tried to remain professional. They were staying in a house in the countryside. From our records, he was sixteen, and his mother was forty years old. The son answered the door; he was wearing a beanie hat, and underneath, it looked like silver foil. He invited us in and showed us into the front room.

His mother was sitting on the couch. She, too, was wearing silver foil on her head. I sat and listened to my mentor interview the two of them. The mother explained that for years now they had been on the run from aliens that were experimenting on them. They wore the silver foil to prevent the aliens from reading their minds and finding out where they were hiding.

"What do these aliens look like?" Dave asked.

"They are like you and me," the woman replied.

"So, how can you tell who is an alien and who is not?"

"It's difficult because they are brilliant at looking like regular people," said the son.

"What would you do if you met an alien?"

The son jumped in hastily and said, "Kill it. We have lots of weapons."

"Okay, can we see these alien killing weapons, please?"

"They're in the car boot, just in case."

They were keen to show us their arsenal of weapons. They opened the boot. There were axes, homemade swords, hammers and steel spikes.

"Thank you for showing them to us. You're not planning on leaving the house this afternoon, are you? I would like to come back and get some more details from you."

"No, we don't go out. My son and I stay indoors as much as we can."

"Okay. Are there any weapons in the house?"

"No, we keep them all in the car in case we need to run."

"Okay, well, thank you for your cooperation. I will pop by later if that's alright with you two?"

"Yes, thank you for dropping by. We will see you later."

They headed indoors, and we headed back to the car. Dave explained the situation and that it was extremely rare for two family members to share the same psychosis. He said that she had probably brought him up like that and he knew no different. He then explained that he would now have to telephone the police and have the weapons seized before they hurt someone. Dave rang the police and met them at the address after dropping me back at the office.

I couldn't help thinking that someone who they suspected of being an alien could have died. They absolutely believed that aliens were hunting them and had been for years. This completely brought home the seriousness of mental health and the impact it can have on an individual.

As far as my next five essays were concerned, I did what Dave suggested and made them up to fit the criteria. The lowest mark I received was seventy-five percent, and the highest was seventy-nine percent.

We were getting to the end of the third year, though since some of the tutors had called in sick and some classes had

had to be mixed, we were down on the number of teaching hours we had to have in order to qualify. I was listening to some of the other students discussing this and there were concerns we might not be allowed to qualify.

This gave me an idea.

I went to see my personal tutor as I needed a piece of university-headed paper. He asked why I needed it; I told him I was going to prank my fellow students one more time before the year was over. He smiled and handed me the headed paper. He too had a great sense of humour and was probably the best lecturer and personal tutor on campus.

I typed out a note to say that we were not having a summer break as we needed to make up the theory time we had missed. There were to be no exceptions and anyone who failed to attend would not qualify and would have to sit the whole third year again. I did it on a Friday morning and thought I would own up to it around lunchtime, after people had possibly stewed over it for a short time. The notice went up and most of the other students did not fall for it, stating that they knew it was me.

Though before the first lecture of the afternoon, the lecturer, who had a sense of humour bypass – as for the three years, they had never smiled, never shared a joke, and heaven help you if you were laughing in any of her lectures – held up my notice and said that she had a lot of students in tears who had come to see her about it. She asked who had done it. I put my hand up and admitted it was me. She asked whether I was aware of the distress and upset I had caused amongst my fellow students. I said everyone knew it was a prank and that they all knew it was me anyway.

I stood up and asked who was upset by it and I would offer my personal apology to them for any distress caused, as that was not my intention. As I looked around the class, people were shaking their heads, and no one owned up to being upset. So, I apologised to the whole class.

The next week, they summoned me to see the Dean. The Dean said that the lecturer had reported me and wanted me dismissed from the course with immediate effect for causing mass upset and for the theft of a piece of headed paper.

"Theft! I can assure you; I stole nothing. I asked for the headed letter and explained why I wanted it. That person who shall remain nameless, as I do not want anyone else to get into trouble, also thought it would be a funny prank if I didn't let it go on too long. The class saw right through it. As I walked into the classroom, they were all saying, 'Nice try. We're not falling for that.'"

The Dean agreed with me luckily. "I have had no reports of 'mass upset' from any of the other tutors. I feel it is basically one tutor who got upset at having to investigate whether it was a prank, and I am not interested in the theft of a piece of paper. I know how much a sense of humour is valuable to nurses. I will have to support my tutor and I will put a letter in your file. And that will be the end of the matter."

I saw my personal tutor and explained what had happened. He said that the tutor who reported me was always complaining about students not conforming to her Victorian attitudes. He also said that the letter would come to him to be put in my file. He said the only file it would go in was the bin.

CHAPTER 6

The best definition of a nurse I saw on the back of a T-shirt. Nurse: Noun - *The first person you see after saying, "Hold my beer and watch this."*

It was finally time. The day had come for my graduation, and I would be qualified to be a nurse. Jane and her parents were attending my graduation. This meant a lot to me as I had been estranged from my own parents for many years. I have never felt prouder of myself than on that glorious sunny day. When I think back, my training had flown by. Although I was feeling ecstatic and pleased with myself that I had graduated as a nurse, suddenly I felt as if I knew nothing about nursing. My last placement had been on an elderly medicine ward and at the end of my placement, they had offered me a job following my graduation.

What is a nurse? You could write a whole library on just trying to explain that one. A nurse is a highly skilled and highly trained person who is there to help you in and out of bed when you are too weak. To give you the medications that you require to get better or to control your ailment. We clean and dress your wounds, remove your sutures and skin clips. When you are feeling afraid, we are there to reassure you and give you the information you need to make you feel better. We also help to look after your asthma, diabetes, COPD and many other conditions you may be affected by. To give your babies their vaccinations, to give you your vaccinations, and the list goes on.

My first day as a qualified nurse was looming. I was terrified; now the real learning would begin.

I had worked on the elderly ward as an HCA and had two placements there as a student, so I knew the staff and they knew me. I settled in well. Sarah was the name of my mentor and overseer. As with any new job, it took my full focus. The first couple of months flew by, and I was finding my feet as a staff nurse.

In my fourth month, I was heading down the corridor towards bay one. Coming the other way was the ward manager, accompanied by two men in suits. The manager beckoned me over.

"Anthony James?" said one man.

"Yes, that's me. How can I help?"

They then introduced themselves as police detectives.

"We are here investigating the potential murder of one of your patients."

It rooted me to the spot. My face drained of colour until it matched the white of my tunic and panic started to set in.

The officer looked at my panicked state and said, "I'm sorry, I could have phrased that better. You are not under suspicion. It is to do with something you witnessed and documented."

"Shall we continue this in my office?" asked the ward manager.

"Again, sorry about the poor phrasing. We didn't mean to worry you. Can you remember a particular old gentleman that you documented in his notes having witnessed his wife hitting him with her walking stick?"

"Ah yes, I entered bay one when I saw his wife hitting him a few times with her walking stick. She said that she was playing and hadn't hit him. I could see by his expression and the force she was bringing the stick down with that she had been serious about hitting him with it. You mentioned murder?"

"Yes, the poor gentleman is dead. She apparently pushed him down a flight of stairs in his wheelchair, and he later died of his injuries."

A cold shiver ran down my spine. "What happens now?"

"It will go to the coroner. You need to attend the court hearing and give your evidence. That will be you reading out what you documented and answering questions the coroner, or the gentleman's family, might have. There is nothing to be worried about. And well done on your observation and documentation. I understand from your manager that you have recently qualified."

"Erm, yes, about four months ago," I said, still trying to comprehend the situation.

"Well, keep up the good documentation. You never know when it might be needed. Thank you. We won't keep you from your work any longer."

Later that morning, the manager came to see how I was doing.

"That must have been a shock for you earlier."

"You're not kidding! I thought for a minute I'd done something wrong and killed someone."

On the day of the inquest, my manager accompanied me to the coroner's court for support. It was not as bad as I thought it might be. They asked me to read out what I had documented. Then the coroner asked if anyone had questions to ask me. Luckily, no one did. I later found out that they dropped the case against his wife, as it transpired that she was suffering from early onset Dementia.

Your documentation will either save you and do you justice, or it may come back to bite you on your arse. If you don't learn anything else, make sure your documentation is accurate, thorough and non-jargonistic.

I had now been on the ward about eight months and had assisted in many ward rounds. Junior doctors came onto the ward, grabbed a patient's notes out of the notes trolley and took them to the patient's bedside, examined the patient, wrote in the patient's notes and left them lying around. I had mentioned this to the consultant frequently about how this was potentially a data protection issue and a breach of confidentiality. Yet these doctors still left the patients' notes lying around, expecting others to clear up after them.

Before the next ward round, I printed off a couple of A4 pieces of paper which read: *ALL Junior Doctors MUST be accompanied by a sensible adult when doing a ward round, or when accessing patients' notes.*

The consultant spotted it first, looked straight at me and slightly shook his head. I merely smiled back and shrugged my shoulders. Then one of the junior doctors spotted it.

"I suppose you think you're bloody funny!" he scolded as he ripped the notice from the side of the notes trolley, then tore it up.

"I placed that notice there. Now, reprint it exactly as I wrote it and place it back on this trolley," said the consultant firmly.

"Erm, I thought…"

"No, you *don't* think. You all act without thinking. These nurses are not here to run after you, or to clean up after you. The next one who leaves a patient's notes lying around for anyone to pick up and read will be in serious bother. Am I understood? And while we are discussing patients' notes, who knows the difference between an autopsy and a biopsy? Because the patient has clearly not 'refused an autopsy'."

The consultant shook his head in despair as he read from a set of notes.

I couldn't believe it. But it worked. They put the notes away from that point on. I developed a good rapport with the consultant. And later, he would always ask if I was on shift to do the ward round with.

I was now working a night shift. The first night went reasonably well. When we arrived for the second night, they informed us that the ladies' six-bedded area was closed for deep cleaning. There were merely three of us on shift that night, as one of the HCAs had rung in sick. That was alright; with six fewer patients being looked after, that would make the night a little easier. The six-bedded area was in front of the nurses' station and partitioned off with large windows above the station area. We had seen to all the patients and got them settled for the night.

There was no one in that six-bedded area, but we kept hearing a noise, like a patient trying to get out of bed. We went to investigate and found nothing. We were all together when we heard the noise again. We went to investigate again. Nothing, we jokingly said. It must be a ghost. At about four in the morning, we were sitting at the nurses' station. All was quiet, and we were contemplating making a drink when there was a loud knock on the window. It startled all three of us; we ran around thinking a confused patient had got out of bed and needed some help. There was no one there. It was a genuinely spooky experience.

About two months had passed, and I was on nights again. This time there were four of us. We told the HCA about our experience. She said it was codswallop and there was no such thing as ghosts. We told her exactly what had happened, and that there was no explanation for it, but she was having none of it. On nights, we used to make a bed in the treatment room. We would place a mattress on top of the physio bed. We weren't supposed to do it, but there was no one around and it happens on all wards at night. Well, it used to back then.

The disbelieving HCA always went to have her sleep break first. I preferred to go last; the night seemed to go quicker that way. I was making the bed up with the other staff nurse when I had an idea. The mattress was about the width of a person, narrower than the actual physio bed, so I pulled the mattress away from the wall. It left a narrow gap; I slipped into the gap and pulled the sheet over myself and the mattress.

"Can you see me?"

"No, it just looks like normal. What are you planning?"

"You'll see." I smiled and said, "It must be time for a drink."

We were all sitting in the dayroom having a coffee when I asked, "Do any of you remove your tops when you have your break?"

"Why do you want to know?" the staff nurse asked.

"I'm merely curious. I always take mine off because this stuff creases like mad and the day staff will know I've slept in it. I just wondered if your tunics creased as bad as these."

The HCA who was going for her break first said that she slept in it as it didn't crease that badly. I then changed the subject to something else, so as not to raise any suspicion.

When it was time to start breaks, the HCA said, "I'm off for a cigarette, then off to bed."

"I'm going to do a ward check," I said.

I told the rest of the staff that I was going to lie in the gap next to the wall and wait for the HCA to come to bed. They said that they would listen at the door to hear what happened.

Several minutes later, I was lying in the gap with the cover pulled over me when I heard the door close, and the light flicked off. I then heard a zipper being pulled down.

Oh, shit. She's taking her top off, I thought to myself. Oh well, too late now.

She climbed into bed and lay down.

Then from the narrow gap, I rolled over towards her and in a deep voice said, "Hello."

She screamed and flew out of bed and landed near the fridge, a good eight feet away. The other two staff members opened the door and turned the light on. The HCA was holding herself up on the fridge with one hand and holding her crotch with the other.

"You silly twat, I think I've pissed myself. *I have*, I've pissed myself."

We were all laughing hysterically. Luckily, she saw the funny side too. However, she still didn't believe in ghosts.

CHAPTER 7

I was asked if I could work on a medical ward for a couple of days as they needed a male presence due to there being a young male patient who, after abusing drugs, was admitted to the ward in need of some medical care. He was being loud and challenging to the female staff, and they thought a male presence may calm him down. I arrived on the ward to find him using the ward phone and being loud and abusive to the person on the other end.

I asked him to be quiet. He glared at me and continued shouting down the phone. I explained that there were extremely ill people on the ward, and he was upsetting them. I told him to lower his voice, or I would unplug the phone. He then told the other person on the phone to fuck off, then hung up.

Two nurses who knew me said they were glad I was on the ward, as they were now feeling quite threatened by the patient. I asked for a handover and update on why he was being admitted and the care he needed. I then went to see him and find out what all the shouting was about.

"Hi, can I have a word?"

"What about?"

"Basically, about your behaviour. The shouting and swearing on the ward. We won't tolerate this. Do you want to tell me what it's all about? Maybe we can help."

"You can't do nowt to help. That was my dickhead brother."

"Okay, what has he done to deserve such a torrent of abuse?"

"He borrowed my car and had it nicked. He's a dickhead. I had that car stolen for me and now he's got it nicked."

"Hang on, you had it stolen for you?"

"Yeah."

"How can it be *your* car then?"

"Cos I had it nicked for me."

"But that doesn't make it your car. It belongs to the person you stole it from."

"It was still my car," he insisted.

He couldn't comprehend that a stolen car did not belong to him. Since he had had it specially stolen for him, he was insistent it belonged to him. Either way, I told him I wouldn't be standing for any more of his unnecessary behaviour.

He remained quiet for the rest of the morning. Shortly after lunch, two uniformed police officers came onto the ward. They asked if we still had the young man on the ward, and if so, could they speak with him, as they had some questions to ask him. I showed them to his bed, but he wasn't there. I said I would go see if he was in the dayroom, but no, not there either. I checked the toilets, but he wasn't in any of them. I told the officers that he may have gone over to the canteen area, so they asked where it was and left the ward. Twenty minutes later, they appeared back on the ward and asked if the young man had come back. I said that I hadn't seen him. They left the ward looking disappointed.

We had not seen him all afternoon, and it was now teatime. We concluded he had seen the police officers and had absconded from the ward. Both myself and an HCA went to change the bed and get it ready for another patient. When we looked in the locker, we found his bag inside. We opened it and found some clothes in there, along with a couple of small bags containing some white pills. Also stashed in a sock was a roll of twenty-pound notes that would have choked a donkey. We informed the police, and later that night, a police officer came to retrieve the bag and its contents. We never saw that young man again.

The next day, I worked on the medical ward again. The previous day's finding was a hot topic of conversation. Though that was now history to the staff, and we had to sort out that day's discharges. There were three of them. One chap in his early sixties was already dressed and packed before breakfast.

"You're keen to get away," I joked.

"Yes, I've had enough of being here. You've all done a marvellous job, but I need to get home and back to normality. The doctor told me yesterday I could go home today."

"The doctor will do a ward round in about an hour. We'll get everything organised for you, get your discharge papers sorted and if the doctor wants you to have any medication to take home, we can get that sorted for you before you go."

"I have a taxi booked for eleven-thirty."

"Okay, we'll try to get everything sorted by then."

This we did, and at eleven-thirty, the taxi driver came onto the ward to collect him. He was in the dayroom waiting patiently. The taxi driver helped him to the taxi and came back for his bags and discharge papers. He collected them and left. Within seconds, the taxi driver came running on the ward and asked if a nurse could see to his passenger as he didn't look well. One of the other nurses went to see to him. Yet minutes later, she too ran back onto the ward, shouting for help. I was seeing to a patient but saw another nurse and two doctors run to her aid.

The poor man had apparently suffered a massive heart attack in the back of the taxi and had died sitting up.

On the acute medical elderly wards, there are quite often a lot of deaths to deal with. They are always upsetting, but, as nurses, we learn to deal with them. Sometimes, seeing the funny side of a situation without being disrespectful can help. We had sadly lost two patients in a single morning. I had helped the new HCA with the last offices. We laid the patients out as their relatives were coming to say goodbye. About an hour before they were due to arrive, the HCA asked what she should do with the false teeth. I said to place them in the mouths of the deceased as this would give their mouths a better shape.

Fifteen minutes before visitations, I asked the HCA if everything was clean and tidy and that nothing had been left lying around. She said no, but she found it difficult putting one of the men's false teeth in. I asked what she meant, and she explained that one of them had been a very tight fit. I went with her to check out the situation. I peered behind the curtain and it looked like he was grinning from ear to ear. I asked her what she had done, and she told me she had put the teeth in the sink and washed both sets together. Unfortunately, she'd got the teeth mixed up and put them in the wrong mouths! We had to hurriedly changed them over before their relatives saw the mistake. All was well in the end.

On a lighter note, one afternoon, myself and an HCA were clearing out an old storage room. Hiding at the back of the room was a medical skeleton hanging from a frame. We cleared out the room and retrieved the skeleton. We had a junior doctor on the ward, so we decided we would put it in a bed and set up a fake intravenous drip. And wait for an opportune moment. We were sitting at the nurses' station writing up some notes when the doctor asked if there was anything for him to do.

"We have a new admission, an anorexic. We think she may have overdone it. We've got her on fluids. She's in room four."

"Okay, I will see her in a minute."

There was an almighty ear-piercing scream from the corridor. We ran to see what the matter was. It was the housekeeper; she had seen the fake name on the room and entered to offer the patient a drink.

"Are you alright?" asked the doctor.

Then we realised which room she had gone into. It was a while before she saw the funny side of it. The doctor was not that impressed either to be honest.

CHAPTER 8

It got to the point where I was now an 'E' grade staff nurse and could take charge of a ward. Back on the medical elderly ward, it was a miserable weekend with heavy rain forecast. Well, at least I was at work and not stuck indoors on a day off with nowhere to go. We had the patients washed, dressed, and had given them their breakfast. There was one old lady we were concerned about, as her condition was gradually deteriorating. One of the HCAs fed her a few teaspoons of porridge. That was all she could eat. It was about ten o'clock when I phoned the 'on-call' doctor who was currently on ward eighteen. This was on the other side of the hospital grounds.

"Hello, ward eighteen, staff nurse speaking."

"Hi, it's Tony on ward five. Can I speak to the doctor, please?"

"Just a sec."

"Hello."

"Hi, Doc, I have an old lady that I'm concerned about; she has deteriorated overnight, and I'd like you to come and have a look at her, please."

"Okay, I'll see what I can do."

An hour had passed, and still no doctor, so I rang him again.

"Hi, I thought you were coming to see my old lady?"

"Erm, yeah, sorry, I'm very busy here. I will get there when I can."

It was now eleven-thirty; I rang the doctor again.

"Hi, Doc, I'm getting concerned about this lady. She appears to be deteriorating further. I would like you to come and see her."

"I can't do anything yet. I'm snowed under over here. I'll come after lunch."

It was still raining heavily, and it hadn't stopped all morning. Lunch came and went and still no doctor. I rang him yet again.

"Hi, Doctor, I am now extremely concerned about this old lady. I must insist that you come and see her, please."

"It's still raining and I'm on the other side of the grounds. I'm not coming yet."

"I'm sorry, but I need you here. This lady has been getting worse all day."

"You do what you like. I'm not coming."

"Okay, I will. Bye."

I then rang the reception to air-call the lady's consultant. The HCA answered the phone then waved me over.

"It's the consultant."

"Hello, it's Tony. I am truly sorry to call you at the weekend, but I have a lady of yours who has been deteriorating all day, and I need her to be seen."

"Where's the on-call doctor?"

"He's on ward eighteen. He told me he's not coming, and I can do whatever I want. So I called you."

"Okay, Tony, give me ten minutes."

I hung up and looked at the clock; it was ten minutes to two. At one minute to two, the on-call doctor burst onto the ward, panting heavily.

"What did you call the consultant for?"

"You told me I could do anything I wanted to. She is his patient, so I rang him. You look soaked. Would you like a towel?" I said, with more than a hint of sarcasm.

The ward phone rang at exactly two o'clock.

"Is he there?" asked the consultant.

"Yes, he looks like a drowned rat, but he's here."

"Please put him on."

"It's for you," I said to the drenched doctor.

I don't know what the consultant said to him, but he saw to the lady, ordering fluids and intravenous medication. Then he wrote up all the drug cards and didn't leave the ward until he had completed everything.

During the consultant's ward round on the Monday, he asked me what had happened on the Sunday. I told him what had transpired and apologised again for disturbing his weekend. I could see he wanted to laugh and appeared to be holding it back when I described what the doctor had looked like when he'd burst onto the ward, soaked to the skin. I thought he might laugh in the end, but he remained extremely professional, though as he turned away from me, there was a definite smile.

Those in elderly care may know the term 'sun-downer'. It refers to how the elderly can become disoriented and agitated at night. This can happen even to patients who seem lucid during the day, but, as the sun goes down, they become disorientated and confused. We had one old gentleman who during the day was well-spoken, polite, and usually sat reading his paper or a book. However, when dusk approached, he slowly changed. He reverted to the Second World War and would pace up and down the corridor or sit in a chair at the end of the corridor near to the nurses' station. When we asked him what he was doing, he replied he was on guard. We would leave him to his own devices as he would not interfere with anything and just sat quietly.

When you train to become a nurse, you are always taught to 'reorient' confused patients. That means informing them that what they think is happening isn't real, and then informing them what is real. This appears to make sense in training, but in the real world, it leads to hours of disagreement with them as to what is real and what isn't real. I have found it's better to step into their world and then steer them out of it. One night when this gentleman was 'on guard', we had a visit from the duty doctor.

He was walking up the corridor when we heard, "Halt, who goes there?"

"It's just the doctor," came the reply in a strong German accent.

"It's a Jerry infiltrator," shouted the old man as he grabbed a fluid stand and charged at the doctor.

I ran towards the old man and shouted, "It's alright, he's on our side."

The old man had the doctor pinned to the wall using the hooks of the fluid stand.

The doctor was great; he got to grips with the situation quickly.

"I'm on your side, I'm friendly," The doctor said calmly.

"Can you identify him?" he asked me.

"Yes, he's on our side. He's one of the good guys."

"You can't be too careful," he said as he lowered the fluid stand and returned to his chair in the corridor.

It was decided to give the gentleman a regular mild sedative to help him sleep at night whilst in hospital as he needed his rest, which he obviously wasn't getting. After that, he slept peacefully all night, every night. When we discussed what had happened, the gentleman could never remember his night-time experiences.

A lot of the time, the elderly patients who are ill can become confused and quite frightened at night. Another night, I heard a noise down the corridor. Someone was rattling the main doors. I went to investigate and saw an elderly gentleman trying to open the door. I asked him what he was doing and suggested we went back to his room. I stretched out my right hand to help guide him away from the door when he suddenly slung something white against my arm. A searing pain shot up my arm, then I found I couldn't move it. One of the other nurses approached us, but I told her to stand back. After some gentle negotiating, we finally got the pillowcase from him. I looked inside and saw it contained the footrest from a wheelchair.

I thought he must have broken my arm. We rang for the on-duty doctor to come see to the gentleman as he was becoming unsettled again. After giving the gentleman a mild sedative, he examined my arm. Luckily, he hadn't broken it. It was the last day of my night shift, so I had a few days to rest my arm, which was lucky.

On my return to work, they informed me that the gentleman that had hit me wanted to speak to me. When he saw me walk into the room, he burst into tears. I asked him why he was upset. He told me that the next day, the doctor had told him what he'd done. He told me he had woken up on the ward and didn't know where he was. He apologised for hitting me and said that he was not a violent person.

After speaking with him for a while, I found out he was a prisoner of war, and he thought that the night he hit me, he must have had a flashback to that time. I told him everything was alright, and that he was frightened and merely protecting himself. Being caring and compassionate is what us nurses do, after all.

People seem to forget that elderly people were once young, vibrant people who led incredible lives. There is a poem that we were given at university to highlight this fact. The poem was written by the daughter of an elderly mum. I was fortunate to correspond with her many years ago. She said she had no idea that her poem would have such impact in the medical profession until she stumbled upon it on my website that I had created to help students.

Crabbit Old Woman
Written By: *Phyllis McCormack*

What do you see, nurse, what do you see?
What are you thinking when you look at me?
A crabbit old woman, not very wise,
Uncertain of habit, with far-away eyes,
Who dribbles her food and makes no reply
When you say in a loud voice, I do wish you'd try.
Who seems not to notice the things that you do
And forever is losing a stocking or shoe.
Who, unresisting or not, lets you do as you will
With bathing and feeding the long day is fill.
Is that what you're thinking, Is that what you see?
Then open your eyes, nurse, you're looking at me.
I'll tell you who I am as I sit here so still!
As I rise at your bidding, as I eat at your will.
I'm a small child of 10 with a father and mother,

Brothers and sisters, who loved one another,
A young girl of 16 with wings on her feet,
Dreaming that soon now a lover she'll meet,
A bride soon at 20 – my heart gives a leap,
Recalling the vows that I promised to keep.
At 25 now I have young of my own
Who need me to build a secure happy home;
A woman of 30, my young now grow fast,
Bound to each other with ties that should last;
At 40, my young sons have grown and are gone,
But my man is beside me to see I don't mourn;
At 50 once more babies play around my knee,
Again we know children, my loved one and me.
Dark days are upon me, my husband is dead,
I look at the future, I shudder with dread,
For my young are all rearing young ones of their own.
And I think of the years and the love that I've known;
I'm an old woman now and nature is cruel
Tis her jest to make old age look like a fool.
The body is crumbled, grace and vigour depart,
There is now a stone where I once had a heart,
But inside this old carcass, a young girl still dwells,
And now and again my battered heart swells,
I remember the joy, I remember the pain,
And I'm loving and living life over again.
I think of the years all too few – gone too fast.
And accept the stark fact that nothing can last
So open your eyes, nurse, open and see,
Not a crabbit old woman, look closer
See Me.

A couple of weeks passed by working on the elderly medical ward, when I was asked by the medical chest ward if I would do some overtime there. They were due an inspection and wanted to prepare for it. I said I would work overtime for them as I enjoyed working on that ward.

Straight after handover, however, the ward manager started running around like a headless chicken, constantly telling us what she needed to be done. We told her everything would be alright, and to calm down, as we still had patients to look after. She wanted the inspection to go well, as anyone would. We cleaned the ward thoroughly and had all the patients' bedside trollies steam cleaned. All treatment areas were sorted out and any clutter tidied away. Everyone worked hard to make sure nothing was left to chance.

I was not working on the day of the inspection but did work on the ward the following week doing some overtime. I asked the nurses how the inspection had gone. They informed me that the inspection team had turned up a day early! Apparently, the ward manager had not been on shift, as she was expecting them the following day. They said she was like an expectant mother, coming on the ward from her office to ask questions about how the inspection had gone. I smiled as an idea entered my head.

I said to the nurse, when we'd got everything done for the patients, I would ring her up and pretend to be the inspector. The rest of the staff thought it would be a fun idea.

I rang from the nurses' station, so we turned the audible alarm off the patients' call system. The board would still light up, showing if a patient was requesting attention. I disguised my voice with a mild Scottish accent. (Many apologies to the Scots as it was a rubbish accent I put on!)

"Hello, is that the ward manager?"

"Yes, how can I help you?"

"My name is Stuart McPherson. I am in charge of the inspection visit that my team came to do a few days ago."

"Ah, hello. How can I help you? I hope you found everything satisfactory?"

"That's why I am ringing you personally. The inspection notes that they have handed to me do not read well, I'm afraid."

"I'm sorry. What do you mean?"

You could hear the concern in her voice.

"Well, the first thing my inspectors found virtually straight away was a soiled incontinence pad laying under a bed. Not the most hygienic of finds."

"We have a few confused patients on the ward, and this can happen, but we always clean everything when we find it."

"My inspectors have written that the pad looked like it had been under the bed for a considerable amount of time, as it did not look freshly soiled. There was also the matter of a used syringe and needle left on the work surface of the treatment room."

"What?! I can't believe my staff would be so careless."

"There was also an opened drug trolley that was left unattended in a four-bedded area, and as you are quite aware, this could have had serious consequences if a patient had helped themselves to the contents of that trolley. Therefore, I think it would be a good idea for us to have a meeting today to discuss the rest of the inspection. I will be on site about two o'clock if that is good for you?"

"Erm, yes. I think we should have a meeting as this is news to me. My staff said everything appeared to go well. I just can't understand it."

"Well, let's leave it there until our meeting. I know you're a busy manager."

"I'll wait for your visit."

I hung up, and we fell about laughing. I hoped that after she found out it was me, she would also see the funny side of it.

We thought she would come onto the ward to find out what had happened during the inspection, but we hadn't realised there was a managers' meeting that morning. Lunchtime came and went as we attended to the patients. It was two o'clock when the afternoon staff came on and had their handover. The ward was quiet, and we had tended to the patients when the ward manager came down the corridor.

"What the hell happened with the inspection? I made sure that everything was done. I now have a meeting with a

Mr McPherson this afternoon. Apparently, the inspection was a disaster," she said in a slightly raised but forceful voice.

"As far as I was aware, everything went really well," said one nurse.

"Well, apparently it didn't."

"Everything was done. The afternoon staff are on, and the ward is quiet. Can we get a flier today?" the nurse asked the manager.

The manager shook her head in disbelief at being asked this question after showing her displeasure at the apparent 'train-crash' of an inspection and reluctantly said, "You might as well. I am not looking forward to this meeting."

"Does that mean Mr McPherson can go early too?"

"What?"

I then put on the fake Scottish accent again.

"Me sister, aye, aboot that meeting. I d'nay think I will attend t'day."

"What? Why are you speaking… you!" (*The penny dropped.*) "You little shitehawk!"

She made a sudden move towards me, but I ran off down the corridor with the ward manager in close pursuit. I had to stop at the main doors as two visitors were entering the ward at that exact moment. She then slapped me on the back of the head. The two visitors looked at her, bemused.

"It's alright, I'm just disciplining the staff."

The two visitors burst out laughing and continued down to the nurses' station.

"And you… well, just watch your back. I couldn't believe what I was hearing. I should have known you'd be behind it."

She breathed a big sigh of relief as the rest of the staff came down the corridor laughing.

"You set of…"

"We don't know what you mean, sister."

You could have a laugh in those days. You would not get away with anything like that now.

CHAPTER 9

I had been working as the 'E' grade for three years when an 'F' grade post on my ward was advertised. I didn't get the role as they gave it to someone they wanted to promote from a different ward. However, because the ward had its full complement of nurses, he couldn't start on the ward until someone left. They therefore offered me to go on some 'F' grade training on different wards at another local hospital. I was going to start my training on their elderly medicine ward. The ward manager of my new ward wanted everyone to work three long days, if possible. He guaranteed that I would not have to work the missing one and a half hours per week but would still be paid the full thirty-seven and a half hours per week. Also, I would never work more than three shifts per week. It worked well. Every few months, I got an extra six days off in a row; it was like having an extra week's annual leave. I learned a lot from this manager and remembered it when I later became a manager myself.

I had been on the ward for six months and winter was now setting in. Winter pressures at the hospital were biting, as there were fewer beds, and winter diarrhoea and sickness was on the increase. We had our fifth patient come down with Norovirus. The manager asked me to put a notice on the ward stating that we were closed to visitors.

I typed out the notice:

The ward is currently closed to visitors because of an outbreak of ~~Diorrear Diarroear~~ ~~Dyerrear~~ **THE SHITS!!**

His face was a picture. "Oh, how I wish we could leave that on the door," he said, laughing. Unfortunately, I had to replace it with a more appropriate one.

We had a student on the ward who was working her final placement. She did not enjoy performing *basic nursing care* duties, cleaning up patients after they had been faecal incontinent. Basically, it was something she was not used to. She would give it a go but turned a lovely shade of green most times. We were still amid the winter diarrhoea and sickness problem, so there would be a lot of cleaning up of patients to do.

I thought I would play a prank on her as she seemed fair game. I appeared from behind a curtain after seeing to a patient. The student was walking towards me when she screwed up her face and pointed to my right arm. Right above my gloved hand was a brown smudge. I looked at it, sniffed it, shrugged my shoulders, and then licked it off. She instantly threw up all over me. My apron took the brunt of the vomit, and my shoes took the rest.

Not the reaction I expected, but I had to live with the consequences of my actions. She was very apologetic, and I said that it was not her fault, but the *Nutella* had tasted nice. I don't think she ever truly forgave me for that, and I can't entirely blame her!

Some patients take to their beds and fulfil the role of the 'sick patient' at visiting times. Even if they are close to being discharged. We do not really know why they do it, but it is a fairly common occurrence. I had noticed that the daughter of a particular patient always fed him a yoghurt when she visited. She said he was too weak to feed himself and asked if we fed him his meals too.

"Nope, we let him feed himself," I said.

"I'm sorry, but he is far too weak to feed himself. That's why I have to feed him his yoghurt."

"He's suffering from Pretendingitis."

"That sounds painful."

"Not yet, but it could be."

"What do you mean?"

"Well, when you find out, you might hit him with the spoon you're feeding him with."

"Sorry, I don't know what you mean," she said.

"There is nothing wrong with your father. He washes and dresses himself and feeds himself. Then when it's visiting time, he takes to his bed. You come in and spoon-feed him yoghurt."

She turned and stared at him. He looked at her, smiled, and shrugged his shoulders. I walked away, chuckling to myself. Some of these patients knew how to wrap their families around their little fingers.

It was now time to change wards again. This time I was going onto the medical neurology ward. What a difference this would be. My first morning on the ward saw the ward manager forcefully kicking a cupboard door closed, which was below the work surface in the treatment room.

"And *you* are?" she asked abruptly.

"I'm your new nurse. I'm to be working here, getting some 'F' grade experience."

"I already have two 'F' grades, so you'll have to watch and see how they work."

She then walked off.

They asked me to admit a young female patient that had arrived onto the ward earlier. I grabbed her paperwork and found her in her bed talking to an older relative. I asked all the relevant questions regarding her and her stay in hospital.

"I think that will do for now, thank you."

"Can I have some water, please?" she asked.

"Of course, I'll bring you a jug now, and can I get your dad anything?"

"I'm her husband."

"Erm, sorry. Can I get you anything?"

"No, I'm fine."

I could not get out of there fast enough.

I had worked on the ward for a couple of weeks when they informed me that a doctor was coming to perform a lumbar puncture for a female patient I was looking after. Later that morning, the young Senior House Officer (SHO) came with a young, extremely good-looking female student doctor. It was hilarious to watch him trying to impress her; it was so obvious.

I stayed with my patient so I could sit with her to talk her through what would be happening. The SHO was explaining about having the patient in the correct position and locating the exact point the needle should enter the spine. The female patient was lying on her left side with her knees tucked up high to her chest. She asked me about the procedure, so I told her that a needle was going to be inserted between the bones in her lower spine. I explained it shouldn't be painful, but she might have a headache and some back pain for a few days. I said it would be especially important that she lay flat on her back for a few hours after the procedure.

The SHO looked at me and said, "Sorry, I thought I was the doctor?"

"The patient asked me what was going to be happening to her, and since you haven't explained it to her, I thought I would."

"So, you are an expert on lumbar punctures; maybe you would like to tell us how it's done?"

I think I had ruffled this peacock's feathers and he wanted to show me up. "Sure."

I stood up and went around to the other side of the patient.

"We need the patient in the foetal position. We can also perform it sitting upright, leaning forward over something like a small table. First, we locate the L3/L4 space by finding the superior iliac crests and placing our thumbs midline to the spine…"

"Right, that'll be fine. Can I carry on now?" the SHO interrupted.

"Sorry, but you asked me. If you get stuck, I'll be just sitting here," I said, winking at the student doctor.

He had been struggling to insert the needle for quite a while, and the patient was becoming distressed by the pain.

I decided that as the advocate for my patient, I would call a halt to the proceedings.

"Okay, Doc, I think you've had enough attempts. My patient is now in pain, and I am calling an end to it for now."

"*You're* calling an end to it?"

"That's right, enough is enough."

"Don't you know who and what I am?"

"To be honest, I don't care who or what you are. I'm calling an end to it."

With a face like thunder, he packed up his equipment and stormed off. The student doctor looked quite embarrassed. I explained that this should be a relatively painless experience for someone to go through and this lady was now in distress. The student doctor looked at her; she was now crying. She apologised for the pain, and I sat talking to her for a few moments. I explained it was not her fault, but eight attempts was somewhat excessive.

Later that afternoon, the ward manager and the consultant asked if they could have a word. They asked me what had happened when the SHO came to perform the lumbar puncture. I said that, in my opinion, he was showing off and trying to be clever in front of the student doctor; I was explaining the procedure to the patient, as he had failed to do so, and she had wanted to know what was happening. I explained that the SHO had asked if I wanted to explain the procedure to the student.

"Performed many lumbar punctures, have you?" asked the consultant.

"No, not one. But it doesn't mean I don't know the principals behind it. Nor have I performed any open-heart surgery, but I needed to be one step ahead of the surgeon in knowing what he might need and when. And after eight attempts to perform the procedure today, I could see my patient was in pain and crying, so I called an end to it. He then asked me if I knew who and what he was. I informed him I did not care who or what he was; I was advocating for the patient who was in distress. Please ask the patient and the student doctor what happened."

"Hmm, quite. Alright, that will be all," said the consultant.

Later that afternoon, the SHO came to apologise for his behaviour and attitude. I said he also needed to apologise to the patient, and he told me that was his next port of call.

The lesson here is to never be afraid to stand up for your patient. Doctors, consultants, they have a job to do. Yes, it is of a more advanced training standard, but they are merely people doing a job and, sometimes, a few need to be reminded of that.

After about six weeks of working days, especially the early shift, it became apparent that there were two factions on the ward. The ward manager and a select few always had the first break, which usually lasted about an hour. The second break usually lasted fifteen minutes. I had witnessed this a few times, as one of those who took the second break. I was sitting with the staff on the second break when one of them said how unfair it was that the manager and her 'followers' had an hour.

I said that if they would back me up, I would try to stop it. I didn't tell them I was good friends with the matron, whose job it was to oversee that particular ward as well as the other medical wards within that hospital. They said they would back me up as they were sick of it.

After about twenty minutes, one of the 'F' grades came in and said we've had long enough and now we needed to get back to work.

"I'm sorry, but we will be back after we have had an hour. You lot have an hour every morning from nine until ten."

"I've been told to come and get you."

"Then come back at eleven. Either you lot have the regulation time for breaks, or we'll have to match the time you have. That's fair, isn't it?"

She was not happy and slammed the door. A few minutes later, the manager came in.

"You lot, out."

"Sorry, we have not had our hour yet," I said.

"OUT! NOW!"

"If we get your assurances that you will split the breaks evenly and both parties will have the same time for breaks, then we'll come back now."

"OUT! I AM THE MANAGER AND I RUN THIS WARD MY WAY."

"Okay, peeps, back to work."

We went back to work, and as the manager came out of the room, she caught her leg on a chair outside the room. She picked it up and threw it down the corridor. I rang the matron and asked if I could have a word after my shift had finished. We made an appointment to see her at three-thirty.

"Hi, Tony, what can I do for you?" the matron asked when we met.

"I would like to bring to your attention the problems on the ward."

"I'm not sure what you mean?" she said, looking surprised.

"Are you aware that there are two factions on the ward? Those that are in the manager's gang, shall we say? And those that aren't. Those in her gang get an hour for their breaks every morning. They often get longer for their lunch breaks too. The others get fifteen minutes for their morning break if they're lucky. Some of the staff have had none of their mandatory training in over three years. The manager kicks the cupboard doors and throws chairs down the corridors."

"I don't believe it," she said.

"I have not come here to lie to you. I thought you knew me better than that?" I started to get slightly annoyed.

"Sorry, I didn't mean I didn't believe you. I just don't believe that this is going on. Why has no one said anything before now?"

"They are too scared to. If or when you interview them, please do it away from the ward. I don't think they will open up properly with the others around."

"What about you?"

"I will put everything I found in writing and will stand up and discuss this in front of them. However, I'm learning nothing on that ward and would like to be moved on at some point."

"That's good to hear. Can I tell them it was you that brought this to my attention?"

"Absolutely. I have nothing to hide."

CHAPTER 10

One week later, they moved me onto a stroke ward. It was about four weeks after that that I bumped into one of the HCAs from the neuro-medical ward. She informed me how different it was now. People were being booked on to their training courses. Breaks were being monitored; the manager was being closely watched. She said it was a much better environment. She also said that people speculated it was me that had informed the matron. I said please go back and tell them the speculation could end, it was me, and tell them I was proud to have done so.

Before starting on the ward, I assumed that strokes merely happened to old or older people. It surprised me that there were a number of young people that were suffering with a stroke. It was a physically hard job, as well as mentally taxing. It was also incredibly rewarding, watching those who had fully recovered after treatment. Due to the sheer nature of the illness, patients were transferred to us on a bed, then a 'Patslide' board was used in order for us to transfer them into a ward bed.

We were receiving patients from AAU who had soiled themselves, both with faecal matter or urination on them. I reported this to the ward manager, who examined the state of the patients coming over from the AAU. Sure enough, he witnessed this; therefore we concluded that this could not have happened in transit as the bed linen was dry when they arrived, so these accidents must have happened a lot earlier.

The ward manager complained to the AAU department, who stated this could not be the case as they checked all patients before leaving their area. The next couple of patients that were transferred over were inspected by the ward manager and he was not happy with what he saw. And so, again, we complained to the AAU department.

The next day, when we had a patient transferred via a bed, the AAU manager came along with the bed. On transferring the patients across into the ward bed, it was obvious that the patients had been urinary incontinent. The bedsheet was extremely stained.

"That must have happened on the way here," the AAU manager said, looking slightly embarrassed.

"Have you come here directly from AAU?" I asked.

"Yes, of course."

"Wow, it must be extremely hot in that lift. This bedsheet is bone dry," I said, shaking my head and looking him straight in the eye.

His face went a dazzling red as he stormed off the ward.

My ward manager walked past the room, so I called her over and explained the situation.

"You mean, after all the shouting that he did, saying that all patients were properly checked before leaving AAU, he brought one up on a soiled bed?"

"Yup. You should have seen his face."

Later that afternoon, a buzzer went off, so I went to see what the patient wanted.

"Oh, erm. Is there a female nurse available? I wish to use my commode," said an old lady.

"I'm sorry, but they're all busy at the moment. I can get one to come soon."

"Erm, I suppose you will have to do as I'm desperate," she said.

I drew the curtains around her bed and helped her onto the commode.

"Press the buzzer when you've finished," I said, giving her the handset.

A few moments later, the buzzer went off. One of the female nurses said she would attend to it. I had to go into the room to replace some intravenous fluids for another patient anyway. The nurse was drawing back the curtains from around that old lady's bed when she called me over.

"Betty, tell him what you just told me."

"I can't do that," she insisted.

"Go on, it will make his day."

"I was telling this nurse that this is the first time a man has taken down my knickers in over twenty years. Maybe I will let you do it again later."

She had an extremely cheeky smile, virtually rivalling my own.

Later that week, we had a patient needing a blood transfusion. The doctor wrote up the appropriate paperwork and we began giving him the transfusion. We explained to him he would have to stay in bed until the transfusion had finished; he was to have three bags of blood, then he was due to have some blood tests. We thought it best to give the first bag late in the afternoon so we could settle him down for the night.

The following morning, we were having a handover from the night shift.

Jenny, the nurse giving the handover, laughed and said something gave the HCA a huge fright.

"What did?" I asked.

"Mr Smith, the chap having the blood transfusion. It was close to midnight, and we were seeing to a patient when we heard an almighty ear-piercing scream. Mr Smith had become confused and somehow got his blood bag off the stand. He had pulled the giving-set out of the bag and emptied the contents of the bag over himself and the bed. When Jane turned around to see who was behind her, she saw him stood there covered in blood. She screamed. She thought he'd cut his throat or something. It looked like something out of a horror film. It took ages cleaning him and the rest of the blood up."

We asked if Mr Smith was alright, but once confirmed, we fell about laughing. It must have been an eerie sight, especially near midnight and with the ward lights turned down.

Later that morning, we sadly lost an old gentleman. They asked me if I would start last offices, and someone could help me later to turn the chap so I could wash his back. A nurse called Susan said she would join me in about ten minutes. I went into the room and two of the curtains were closed. I went to bed two as that was where I'd been told the chap was. I put the bowl of ward water on the locker, wetting and soaping the flannel. I pulled the sheet down and as I placed the flannel on his chest, both his eyes suddenly opened.

"Oh, I am so sorry. I thought you were someone else," I blurted out.

He didn't move, so I gave him a gentle nudge. My heart was pounding. I thought I had started washing someone who was still alive. It gave me such a shock that as soon as the flannel touched his chest, both his eyes had opened.

A patient was being transferred from another ward who had been admitted with a suspected stroke or mini stroke. He was in his eighties and confused. We had been seeing to his needs when a staff nurse and a student nurse came onto the ward. They said they had brought the rest of his medication, including an injection that he regularly had in his gluteal muscle. The doctor had said it was alright to administer the injection and could the student nurse deliver the injection as part of the competences for her workbook.

I said that would be okay, but it would be better with him on the bed laid on his side. We positioned the chap on the bed and the student was standing in front of him.

"I think it would be better if you stood behind him to deliver the injection."

"I'm a third-year student. I think I know how to give an intramuscular injection."

"The gentleman is confused, and standing around the back would be much better."

Well, she knew best. After all, she was a third-year student. She delivered the injection and at the same, he thrust his free hand straight up her dress. She jumped back and called him a dirty old man and slapped his hand.

"My office now!" I said firmly.

The staff nurse looked at her and shook her head.

In my office, I let loose.

"One, you are a student nurse, and when a trained nurse tells you it is better to do something in a particular way, it's for an extremely good reason and you should listen. Two, never let me see you assault a patient again. You were told to stand behind him. No, you knew best. After all, you're a third-year student, you know everything. That poor man is confused, possibly afraid. He shouldn't have done that, but if you had done what I had suggested, it would not have happened."

I turned to the staff nurse. "I hope this incident goes into her workbook."

The staff nurse apologised and stated that it would go into her workbook, along with a few comments about the incident.

I later spoke with the staff nurse again. She informed me that the student definitely had an attitude problem and they had reported this to the university. I don't know what happened to that student, but I hope she learnt her lesson.

I had supposedly been working towards my 'F' grade for approximately eighteen months. Every time I asked if there was going to be a re-grading of my role, I kept getting told there was no money yet, but I still needed to be working at that grade. I was now feeling like I was being taken for a mug. Working as an 'F' grade but being paid as an 'E' grade.

I was looking on the NHS jobs website when an 'F' grade job appeared in a local prison. I discussed the post with my manager, who said that she wanted me to stay on the ward. I asked again about re-grading and was told again that there was no money.

I have nothing to lose, I told myself and applied for the job. The interview appeared to go well. Later that evening, I received a telephone call from the matron that had interviewed me. She asked me how I thought I had done at the interview. I told her I had felt comfortable and answered all the questions as thoroughly as I could. She informed me I did well; however, I was narrowly pipped at the post by a nurse that was already working in the prison and obviously had prison experience. She then told me she would be looking to appoint a manager and said I should apply for that.

I said I would give it some thought. The post was eventually put on the NHS jobs website. I thought, *well, if I didn't get the 'F' grade, how the hell am I going to get the 'G' grade position?* I thought, *what the hell*, and applied anyway. The interview again went well, and I fully answered all the questions.

The matron rang later that day and asked how I thought I had done. I said that I felt I had done well. This time they offered me the post. I couldn't believe it! I got the job on the proviso that all my security checks and references came back satisfactory, which they did, of course.

I wrote out my resignation and handed it to my manager.

"You got the 'G' grade job?"

"Yes."

"Well done. But I would rather you'd stayed here."

"There's no promotion on the horizon here, and unfortunately, I have to do what is best for me."

CHAPTER 11

I was apprehensive about working in a category B prison, mainly because of having never worked in one before. Although, I was looking forward to my first day. The director of nursing I would be working with met me at the main gate. I would have to do a prison induction course, which lasted two days.

The matron showed me around the prison and introduced me to the staff and the other people I would be working with. I soon made friends with the prison staff on the wings I would work on. My job was to help the matron in setting up an effective healthcare system for the prisoners. This would not be an easy task. Normally, in a hospital or GP setting, they would be a patient first-and-foremost. But, in prison, they needed to be treated as a prisoner first, and a patient second. This would make delivering healthcare more difficult. We would basically have a couple of hours in the morning and a few in the afternoon to deliver the care needed.

For the first few months, I was finding my feet, and the time flew by in an instant. I had various projects to work on and complete, meetings to attend, which were mainly outside of the prison. This kept me busy and out of trouble. The matron knew her role well; I enjoyed working and learning from her.

The one thing that shocked me was the high level of mental health issues within the prison. There were prisoners within the establishment who, in my humble opinion, should never have been in there. These were prisoners with mental health problems who would have been housed in the mental health facilities that were now closed down. These were 'poor copers'. They were in prison because they had committed a crime, but being in prison was the one safe sanctuary for them.

When it got close to their release dates, they didn't want to go. I would see some of them at the drugs hatches and talk to them about their release. They often said that they would be back in prison the week following their release. When I asked why, they said that there was nowhere on the outside where they felt safe or they could get immediate help. One told me he would commit a crime, then when it went to court, he would insult or threaten the judge. This would guarantee a longer sentence. I found this incredibly sad.

There was a prisoner who had a nasty thigh wound. It was an open wound that he didn't want to heal. It was that bad that his thigh muscles were clearly visible. We even tried negative pressure wound care. Negative pressure wound therapy is a procedure in which a vacuum dressing is used to enhance and promote wound healing in acute, chronic wounds. The therapy involves using a sealed wound dressing attached to a pump to create a negative pressure environment in the wound. He would regularly sabotage our efforts.

We later found out he was earning a lot of money transporting drugs around the prison, secreting them in between his thigh muscles. What price would you put on a limb? Even when we informed him he could lose his leg, he would say he could at least afford a wheelchair.

One day, while working in one of the treatment areas handing out medications, a prisoner came to the hatch and asked for some paracetamol to be kept in his cell as he was suffering from a bad headache. They classed this as a 'green drug', a safe drug they could have in their cells.

Then another prisoner came and asked the same thing. He, too, was given a small amount of paracetamol to take to his cell. Then a third prisoner came and asked for paracetamol for his bad headache.

"What's going on? Why are you all having bad headaches?"

"I don't know, guv; can I have some?"

"You can take two here, but you cannot have any to take to your cell. Drink plenty of water; you might be suffering from dehydration. If you still have a headache this afternoon, you can have another couple of tablets to take at the hatch."

"But, guv, you've given them some."

"Sorry, but we will not be handing out any more paracetamol."

We reported this suspicious activity to the prison and later learned that they had been crushing it up to an extremely fine powder, heating it over some silver foil until it turned a light brown in colour. Then they were selling it to other wings as heroin. We never found out if it was being cut with any heroin, merely that it was supposedly being passed off as heroin.

Sat in my office one morning, I received a phone call from a wing, asking if a nurse could come to the wing and do a sick call as there were several prisoners refusing to go to work or education because of various illnesses. I informed them I did not currently have a nurse free but would come myself.

The officer showed me into the first cell. The young man was still lying on his bed when we entered the cell. I asked what the matter was; he said he had a bad back and could not go to work. The officer told him to get off his bed, so he got off his bed and stood up with no sign of pain. I noticed his tatty trainers by the side of the bed. I asked if I could see them. He bent down and picked them up without hesitation.

I informed the officer that this prisoner was fit for work. We then moved on to the next cell. I asked him what he was suffering with.

"I just feel shite, guv."

"Describe your ailments to me."

"I'm hot and sweaty, headache. I just feel shite, guv."

After an examination, his temperature was normal, his blood pressure was normal, a check of his blood sugars was also normal. I gave him two paracetamols, told him if he still had a headache this afternoon, he could have some more. Declared fit for work. I also declared the next two prisoners fit for work. Then we entered another cell.

"What seems to be the matter with you?"

"I can't go to education; I can't read and write properly and the rest of them just take the piss out of me. I get depressed."

"Learning to read and write would be of great advantage to you when you get out of prison. You can go to art class for now. Express yourself and paint."

I knew this prisoner had some mental health problems, and he was being bullied. He was due to be released in a few days' time, so I asked the officer if they could keep him in his cell until they released him back into the community. They agreed.

Later that afternoon, a wing officer came to see me and informed me they had alerted the prison security that the prisoners on the wing had issued me with a death threat. They took these things seriously, so they would escort me on and off the wing for the sick parade the next morning.

"Sorry, but that will just make me look weak."

"We have to take these things seriously, even if we feel it's merely bravado."

"Okay, then have the officers doing something on the wing, strategically placed, when I come on at nine o'clock tomorrow morning. But you will not escort me on or off the wing. I won't show weakness and be exploited."

"I don't think for one minute it's a genuine threat, but we must take it seriously. We'll arrange to have a couple of officers talking to the prisoners on the ground floor."

"Okay, thanks."

The next morning, I went back onto the wing for sick parade. I nervously walked onto the first floor of the wing just in case the threat was a genuine one. I shouted out if anyone wanted to attend for sick parade. No one stepped forward. I calmly walked off the wing and back to my office. I was a little nervous, but thankful it appeared to be an empty threat. I was not going to show any weakness that some prisoners would then try to exploit. Prisoners are always looking for ways to exploit the system to gain the upper hand. Showing any form of fear could lead to them blackmailing you into small acts of corruption. Which would eventually lead to bigger things.

I was enjoying working at the prison, getting to know some of the prisoners. Some were merely fools who had mixed with the wrong sort and had been led astray. Some, on the other hand, were career criminals. One lad who had done a lot of burglaries taught me a lot about how to keep your house safe and what locks *not* to buy. He said to look at the back of some locks; the packaging shows the internal workings of the lock; he said it's a gift for the burglar to work out how to pick it.

Although I was managing the prison outpatient department, I had also been recently required to work two clinical sessions per week. After my latest personal review, I was informed that I was not punitive enough with my staff. I questioned why. I was told that my staff were walking around the prison in twos when they should be working alone. I asked why this mattered as they felt safer and were supporting each other. Also, their work was being carried out to a high standard. Everything I asked them to do they did. So why should I have to be punitive? I have always said, treat your staff well, and they will go above and beyond. Some old-fashioned managers just can't see that.

The higher management asked me to step in at a GP surgery as two nurses had recently left under a cloud, and this meant they were short of a practice nurse; it was to be for three months until they employed a couple of replacements. However, the three months turned into six months. Six months turned into twelve months, and in the thirteenth month, low and behold, the new healthcare manager and the new modern matron came to see me.

Basically, they said we've done without you for thirteen months, so obviously we do not need you (nicely stabbed in the back). They said I had two choices. I could stay where I was or look for another job. Yes, it was as cold as that. There would not be an interview. As far as they were concerned, the meeting never took place, and I was to take the offer or leave and find another job.

I couldn't believe what I was hearing. In the end, I took the job and stayed there; it was going to be fun working with two great nurses, but there was to be a lot of bullying along the way from the nurse manager, which would cause a lot of good nurses to leave various posts around the city.

CHAPTER 12

To begin with, there was me and another nurse called Julie. We worked together well. Soon there was another nurse, Louise. Her nickname was 'Dipsy' and still is. We formed a great friendship that we still have to this day. It would not be wrong to say we ran that surgery between us. We ordered stock, sorted holidays out between us, hit all our targets. The three of us working together rocked. I would also get to play tricks on them, too, which made it all the better.

Louise was a little on the gullible side, an extremely good, caring, knowledgeable nurse, but also gullible. Would I prey on that part of her personality? You bet I would! But more of that later...

Our staff room was upstairs and equipped with a fridge, microwave, kettle, etc. We would put our lunches in the fridge, store milk in there, and sometimes, the women would store some shopping in there, if they had nipped out at lunchtime. Then one day, Louise said that someone had opened some ham she had bought that lunchtime. I said it was definitely not me. I would never do such a thing, not even as a prank.

Then someone else reported that someone had done the same to them and their lunch that they had brought in from home was stolen from the fridge. Even drinks weren't safe. I bought a large bottle of cloudy lemonade, which appeared to be the favourite target. I emptied some out and loaded it with citric acid; it would be vile. It was in the fridge for a couple of days before someone helped themselves to a glass of it.

That did the trick. After that, it was rare that something went missing from the fridge. Whilst we are discussing fridges, we all had fridges in our clinical rooms, which contained injections and vaccines of various descriptions. We recorded these temperatures twice per day. I had gone into Louise's room for something, and she asked me if I had seen the temperature folder. I said I hadn't and asked when and where she had last had it. She said it had been on the top of the fridge. This was a small fridge, so lots of things got placed on the top of it.

Yet we could not find the folder anywhere, so I peered down the back of the fridge. There it was. It had fallen down the back. We cleared the fridge and I helped her pull it out. It was a tight fit, so we had to wiggle it out. Eventually, we got the fridge out and retrieved the folder. Putting the fridge back was a bit more difficult. There was a slight lip at the back that the fridge needed to be lifted on to. I could not get any purchase on the fridge, so opened the door to hold the top and tilt it forward whilst pushing it back into place. I was doing this on my own as Louise was filling something in. She turned around to see the fridge door open, so she tried to close it. It wouldn't close, so she slammed it harder. I stared at her in disbelief as she slammed it again even harder.

This time I shouted, "Ouch!"

She looked down to see why the fridge door wouldn't shut. I still had my fingers in it. All Louise could do was laugh. There was a deep crease across my fingers where the door had hit them. I promised I would get my revenge. She was, and still is to this day, a walking disaster area.

Later that day, I was cleaning out the storeroom when I came across some out-of-date condoms that needed to be thrown away. Louise was getting ready to go home and had put her coat on. It had the hood folded down at the back. I sneaked about twenty condoms into her hood and watched as she left the building. I didn't know it, but she was actually going to see her mum straight after work!

The next day, Louise came to see me in my room. She said that when she'd got to her mother's house, she'd taken her coat off and all these condoms had come raining down out of her hood. She said her mother had asked what they were. When Louise had noticed they were condoms, she'd panicked and picked them up as fast as she could and diverted the conversation away from the condoms. Louise said she'd been mortified when all the condoms fell out. All I could do was smile and chuckle at the vision of it. But she would get her revenge a few days later.

We were sitting in the staff room and had started eating our lunches. I was sitting at the back of the table. Behind me was a long couch-like seating area. In walked Louise, and she sat to my right at the table. She then produced a hard-boiled egg from her lunchbox and hit me square in the middle of my forehead with it. I thought she had hit me with a brick; I reeled backwards, and the back of the chair gave way. I fell backwards through the chair and landed on the couch area. The two metal arms that the backrest used to be attached to now pinned me into the chair. I couldn't move. I lay there struggling to get up, with everyone laughing at me.

"What did you do that for?" I asked.

"I needed something solid to crack my egg on," came her reply.

Eventually, they relented and helped me back up.

We had a computer system which let us know who was attending our individual clinics and why they were coming to the surgery. If Louise or Julie had blank spaces, I would put in fictitious patients like Hugh Jarce, Anna Bolic, Connie Lingus, E. Rex Sean, Helda Dick. Sometimes, the reception team would put patients in to see the nurse when they actually needed to see a doctor. It could be quite frustrating for the nurse and the patient, who could end up having a wasted journey if the doctors couldn't see them at that time.

I put a patient in Julie's clinic, Emma Royds, with a reason for the visit as 'bleeding piles.' Julie spotted this lady should not see her, but a doctor. Not happy that the reception team had done this, she went downstairs and complained to the reception staff that it was an inappropriate booking. It needed to be changed to a doctor immediately.

The reception team looked at the booking and laughed.

"What's so funny?" asked Julie.

"Have you not read the patient's name?" came the reply.

"What do you mean?"

"Look at the screen and read it out loud."

"Emma… Royds. EmmaRoyd… Haemorrhoids. I'll kill him! I am so sorry."

The reception team saw the funny side. Julie forgave me in the end, after she'd cooled off…

Some patients are up for a laugh, especially the elderly. I remember one lady I saw regularly, who we will call Doris. She was always in a wheelchair due to very poor mobility, but this didn't affect her sense of humour. She said that there was always someone worse off than you. She invariably had a joke and a smile for the nurses. When the flu season was about to start, we had a flu clinic set up on a Saturday morning. We had several nurses and doctors administering flu vaccines. This allowed us to get most of our patients vaccinated quickly in one day. On this day, my workstation was next to Louise's, so we would tease each other and generally lighten the mood for our patients. I spotted Doris in the queue and gave her a wave. As we worked our way down the queue, Doris ended up going to Louise.

"Oh, I see. You've dumped me as your nurse then," I said. "They can't like you very much if they've sent you to see her," I said sarcastically and nodded my head in Louise's direction.

"Don't mind him, you're seeing a real professional today," said Louise as she poked her tongue out at me.

Louise then asked Doris all the safety questions before turning away to prepare the flu vaccine. As she did, I mimed to Doris that after the injection, she should pretend to faint. Doris nodded. Louise administered the injection and a couple of seconds later, Doris rolled her eyes and flopped back in her wheelchair.

"Oh my God, Doris, are you okay?" Louise said, giving her a little shake of the shoulders.

"Have you killed another?" I said as the queue now looked over in our direction.

Doris opened her eyes and said, "He made me do it!"

"I'm going to kill him later. You scared the life out of me!"

The people at the front of the queue started laughing as Louise squirted water at me. We are still very good friends and can laugh about that moment today.

They asked me to cover at another surgery as they were short staffed because of illness. My clinic was full, and they kept me busy. I got an 'on-screen' message. It asked if I could see an Asian lady whose recent caesarean scar was causing her pain. I said that I would look at it as it could be an infection. Being an Asian lady, I asked if she knew she would be seeing a male nurse. They said they had told her the nurse was a man, and that she didn't mind as the pain was bad. I asked them to send her straight down as I didn't have a patient in. There was a light knock on the door.

"Come in."

An Asian lady entered the room, rubbing her belly. "Not much English, sorry," she said nervously.

"You have pain?" I asked, pointing to my belly.

"Yes, much pain."

"Okay, if you are happy for me to have a look, please go behind the curtain and get yourself ready."

I finished what I was doing on the computer and the lady went behind the curtain. After a couple of minutes, she shouted she was ready. I put on my apron and gloves and went around the curtain. The lady was lying there, totally undressed from the waist down, knees pulled up and open. I stood there for a second, wondering what was going on, then she started saying "bad pain" and pointing to her vagina.

It wasn't a caesarean; she had had an episiotomy. I didn't want to embarrass the lady, so I had a quick look and couldn't see anything out of the ordinary. I hadn't examined anyone post-episiotomy before. I said to the lady that I thought it looked fine, but I would get the doctor to make sure.

I covered her modesty with poly-roll and went in search of a female doctor. I explained to the doctor what had happened, and she fell about laughing at my embarrassment. She examined the lady and saw nothing that could cause her the pain she said she was suffering. The doctor made her another appointment the following week as a follow-up and prescribed her some pain relief.

I was back to my surgery on Monday.

If two of the three of us or the three of us were together in one of our clinic rooms, we always spoke close to a whisper, as there were two managers that loved to listen at the door. We caught them out several times, and their excuse was, "I was listening to see if you had a patient in with you." At breaks and lunchtimes? Really?

Louise came to see me in my room one day, and we were putting the world to rights when we heard the door to the corridor squeak open. Then nothing. We didn't hear the doctors' door open or close, or the fire escape door, which was used as a shortcut to the car park. Louise whispered that there was someone listening at the door. I said I don't think so and blurted out, "I don't care who's listening at the door. They will only hear the truth."

Louise tiptoed over to the door and promptly opened it. The nurse manager literally fell into the room.

"Erm… I was purely listening to see if you had a patient in with you," she stuttered.

"What, for over five minutes? It doesn't take that long."

She told us she was on annual leave for the next week and left the room. We watched our backs from then on. The situation at the surgery was getting worse and Julie asked me if I had the number for the pensions team as I had already taken early retirement and had gone back down to three days per week. I gave her a number to ring for HR and insisted that she had to ask for a helpful lady called Liz.

A couple of days later, Julie came down to see me. She even called me a few choice names.

"What's the matter?" I asked.

"You know very well what the matter is, you swine. I rang that number and a posh woman answered. I asked if I could speak to Liz. She said there wasn't anyone there called Liz. I told her that I had been given this number and to ask for a helpful lady called Liz, who would be able to help with information about retiring. The posh woman then said you have called Buckingham Palace." I couldn't keep a straight face.

It was not long after that that Julie had to retire because of ill health. Then Louise left because she could no longer take the harassment and bullying from a particular manager. Sadly, I eventually left for the same reason. As they say, you can run, but you can't hide. How true that would turn out to be.

CHAPTER 13

I took a post working for another GP surgery close to where I lived; it was a great surgery, and I was loving it there. I had been there about four months when they informed me that the surgery was to be taken over by the company I had recently left. My heart sank.

I received many text messages saying things like: She's got you now, there's no escape from her, watch your back. They had seen the bullying from before, not solely against me, but many others. From my face-to-face reviews, it was clear that she was making life difficult for me. Every review was negative, despite all the positive stuff from patient letters stating that I had saved their life, as well as the abundant feedback cards that my patients had filled in. So, I collected all the evidence I could. Evidence with times and dates.

Then, out of the blue, a manager of nursing came to see me at the surgery. She asked if she could have a private word with me. So, we went down to my clinic room. She asked if there was anything wrong and if I was alright.

I said, "Yes, I'm fine."

She then repeated her question. I figured she must know something. I told her what I was about to do, then her mood and manner changed. She told me that this lead nurse was the best we had and that she was not a bully, as she was always saying good things about the nursing staff at meetings.

She was adamant that she was not a bully, as she showed no signs of being one. I said, "You have never heard the expression kiss up, slap down?"

"What do you mean?"

"Bullies will kiss up, always say the right things to those above them, whilst slapping down all those under their management or who are subordinate to them. Why are you ignoring all the complaints about her? This is a prime example."

"I am telling you; she is not a bully."

It was at that point I said that we had better end the meeting as I may say something we might regret. She then told me that if I mentioned anything about this meeting to anyone, I would have her to deal with.

Well, as a nurse, we are told to do a lot of reflection, so while it was fresh in my mind, I wrote it all down, but left out her name. Then I sent it to my union representative.

That was it, enough was enough. I then made an appointment to see the 'speak-out guardian' and presented all the evidence I had collected. She read through it and asked if the CEO could see some of it. I said I didn't have a problem with that. I didn't keep it a secret what I was doing, but unbeknown to me, others took advantage and put their complaints in too.

I had a meeting with the person who was conducting the investigation, and they asked who the manager was that had threatened me in my room. I said that as long as I was working for the company, I would not divulge her name. That was something I later regretted.

They carefully looked at the complaints and whilst they were investigating them, they suspended the lead nurse pending the outcome of the investigation.

Unfortunately, they did not dismiss her. I knew she was never to do my personal reviews again. However, she was extremely controlling, and those who were carrying out my evaluations had questions that could only have come from her. Sadly, it was time to move on again. It is never easy, but if anyone is in a similar situation as I was, my advice is to collect evidence, times and dates, and when you have enough evidence, do not be afraid to use it. Don't put up with bullying.

I found a job straight away and left that company yet again. This new job was fantastic. They appreciated the work I did. There was no one spying on me. The reception staff were kind and helpful. I'm still working there today. We have grown into a small family group. We help and look after each other, and it is a pleasure to go to work and not fear being bullied.

On a lighter note, an eighty-four-year-old lady came in for an asthma review. She asked if it would be alright if her daughter came in with her.

I said, "Of course. Where is she?"

She told me her daughter had dropped her off and was parking the car and wouldn't be long. I suggested we get started and her daughter could come in when she returned. I was explaining the procedure for her 'peak-flow'. We perform this using a small, hand-held device that monitors a person's ability to breathe out air. It measures the flow rate of a person's maximum speed of expiration. You put your mouth around a cardboard tube and blow hard.

There was a knock at the door. It was the lady's daughter. I said come in and asked her to take a seat.

"Is everything okay, Mum?"

"Yes, the nurse was just explaining how to give him a blow job."

My jaw hit the floor. The daughter looked at me and said, "I'll step outside and leave you two to it, then."

The old lady laughed and said, "Have I to take my teeth out?"

I looked at the daughter, who was staring at me. "She means a peak-flow. She needs to blow into this tube," I said, embarrassingly.

The daughter now burst out laughing.

"What are you laughing at?"

"It's alright, Mum, I'll explain later."

I don't know if the old lady had deliberately said what she did, but she had a cheeky grin.

Another embarrassing situation involved my chair. The casters kept sticking and it would not roll forward properly and used to suddenly stop dead in its tracks. I had a young lady in for a diabetic review and had finished examining her feet when I tried to shift my chair forward. The chair refused to move. My bottom slid forward to the front of the chair, causing it to tip forward. The chair suddenly shot backwards. As I flew forwards, my head landed straight between her legs. As I scrambled to get up, I fell forward again, with my head hitting her in the crotch. I got up and apologised, my face redder than a post-box. She luckily laughed it off and asked if I was alright. The only thing I had hurt was my pride.

Another time, I had an old lady suffering with stomach cramps. I gave her a sample pot and asked her to bring in a stool sample. I was not in the surgery the day she brought her sample in. The reception staff told me she had come up to the desk and said I had asked her to bring in a stool sample. They said it was fine, and that they would see to it and send it off. The old lady reached into her bag and pulled out a pudding basin.

"What's that?" the staff member asked.

"My stool sample."

"Were you not given a special pot?"

"Yes," she replied.

"Why did you not use the pot?"

"I couldn't get it all in. It's only a small pot."

The receptionist gagged as she explained what she should have done and asked the old lady to go to the toilet and take a small sample using the spoon inside the sample pot.

You cannot always trust that when a patient states they fully understand what procedure they are attending for, that they do understand.

Also, patients tend to write what they are thinking, and do not realise that the written word does not always match what they really meant to say, nor do they tend to take particular notice of their spelling. At the surgery, we have feedback cards that patients can fill in to say how good or how bad we have been doing. We discuss these at team meetings and then send them off to our main office for evaluation of the surgery's performance.

'I enjoy coming to see Tony because I never feel it when he puts it in.' (She was referring to a needle when taking her blood, honest.)

'Saw the male nurse today. He always genital with me.'

'This will have to be short as ink in my penis running out.' (Always watch your spacing.)

I volunteered to do several Covid vaccination clinics at a local centre. I knew the nurses that I would be working with, and we all got on great. We turned what could be a monotonous role into something fun and enjoyable. We also had a bit of a competition between us to see who could vaccinate the most people per shift, safely of course. The nearer to lunchtime it got, the slower it became. We would be stood around waiting for people to inject, then battle to see who would be the one to vaccinate them. One morning, close to lunch, there were four of us waiting for the next person to arrive. We heard a noise down the corridor, letting us know someone had arrived late for a vaccination. The four of us stood posing in a line, when this old lady appeared in the doorway. Claire, one of the nurses, asked the lady, "Who would you like to vaccinate you?"

The lady looked at us all before pointing at me. I strutted forward and held my arm out to escort the lady to my bay.

"Sorry, can I just ask why you chose him over me?" asked Claire.

"Because he looks more my age," the old lady replied.

"Just out of interest, how old are you?" asked Claire.

"I'll be eighty-five next month."

Everybody fell about laughing, and they will not let me forget it.

Amongst my treasured possessions is this letter. A patient I had got to know whilst working at one of the surgeries came in for a regular review. Visual observations of your patients can reveal a lot. He came in looking pale and appeared breathless. Something unusual for him. I asked him how he felt and just like most of the older generation, he replied that he was fine. The nurses' 'Gut Feeling' kicked in. I recorded his basic observations of blood pressure, pulse, respirations, took bloods and decided that an ECG would also be an appropriate action to take. Without going into detail, the results all pointed to a possible trip to the hospital. I wanted to run the results past one of the doctors for confirmation. The doctor said that he would see the patient a little later that morning. About six weeks later, I was given an envelope addressed to me.

A FEW 'DAD' JOKES TO KEEP YOU SMILING.

- Last week my wife wanted to play doctors and nurses. I strapped her to a trolley and left her in the hallway for 8 hours. (Anon).
- The nurse who can smile when things start to go wrong… is the one going off duty. (Anon).
- I got a phone call last night to say that my wife had been in an accident. I rushed to the hospital and asked the nurse, "How is she, can I see her?" She looked at me sadly and said, "I'm afraid you're too late." I said, "Okay, no problem. I'll come back in the morning." (Anon).
- A Covid test nurse asked me if I've had a sudden loss of taste. I told her, "No, I've dressed like this for a long while." (Anon).
- My dad got his Covid vaccine in the top of his leg. His Pfizer killing him. (Anon).
- Never challenge Death to a pillow fight. Unless you're prepared to deal with the Reaper cushions. (Anon).

I hope you have enjoyed reading this book as much as I have enjoyed writing it. There is so much more I could have put in this book, but some things are better kept a secret.

GLOSSARY

A flier – finishing your shift early before your actual finishing time.

Air-call – a small radio device, activated from a central point, which emits a series of bleeps or vibrates to inform the wearer that someone wishes to contact them.

CPR – stands for **cardio-pulmonary resuscitation**.

ECG – an **electrocardiogram** is a simple test that can be used to check your heart's rhythm and electrical activity.

Last offices – relates to the care given to a body after death.

R.N. – a registered nurse.

Shroud – a garment in which a dead person is wrapped.

Sluice room – a room for the disposal of bodily waste and testing urine samples.

Sputum pot – A sterile clear plastic specimen pot with a screw top, used for collecting sputum samples.

Printed in Great Britain
by Amazon